DISCIPLINE

FOR HOME AND SCHOOL

BOOK ONE

REVISED AND EXPANDED EDITION

EDWARD E. FORD

Introduction by John Champlin

National authority on school restructuring

Foreword by William T. Powers

Originator of perceptual control theory
Author of *Behavior: The Control of Perception*

Brandt Publishing

Cover Design: Dorothy Ford Johnson, Phoenix, AZ
Cover Photograph: Steve Thompson, Cavecreek, AZ
Design & Typesetting: Greg Williams, Gravel Switch, KY
Printing & Packaging: O'Neil Printing, Phoenix, AZ

ISBN 0-9616716-6-1

Library of Congress Catalog Card Number: 97-076799

Revised and Expanded Edition

Printed in the United States of America

5   4   3   2   1

Brandt Publishing
10209 North 56th Street
Scottsdale, AZ 85253
602-991-4860

Contents

Acknowledgements ... *ix*
Introduction
    by John Champlin ... *xii*
Foreword
    by William T. Powers ... *xiv*
A Word of Caution about Starting the Program ... *xvii*

Part 1. The Basics of RTP

  1. What This Book Is All About ... *1*
  2. A Simple Understanding
     of Perceptual Control Theory ... *6*
  3. What Is Discipline? ... *13*
  4. When Should Discipline Be Used? ... *15*
  5. Establishing Discipline ... *17*
  6. When Are Children Willing to Learn Discipline? ... *20*
  7. Setting Rules and Standards ... *28*
  8. What Should Happen
     When Children Break Rules? ... *31*
  9. Techniques for Getting Children to Think ... *42*
10. When Children Want to Solve Their Problems ... *52*
11. Dealing with Children
     Who Continually Break Rules ... *64*
12. Knowing Your Limitations ... *74*
13. Keeping the Program Alive ... *78*
14. Dealing with Objections ... *82*
15. Thoughts from Educators Who Helped Implement
     This Discipline Program ... *89*

Part 2. Practical Advice

16. How Did We Do It?
     by Ed Snyder and Wendy Thomas ... *100*
17. Thoughts and Suggestions from an RTC Teacher
     by Darleen Martin ... *107*
18. Dealing with Students Who've Been Fighting
     by George Venetis ... *117*

19. The Responsible Thinking Process,
the Special Needs Child, and
Special Education Mandates
by LeEdna Custer-Knight ... *133*
20. RTP and the Pre-School and
Primary Special Education Classrooms
by Carmen Duron and Erin Powell ... *139*
21. Challenges with Special Ed Students
by Mark Hamel ... *160*
22. An Alternative for Challenging Students
by Bobbie Hodgins ... *168*
23. Juvenile Corrections and RTP:
How It Works at Catalina Mountain School
by Bill Lackman ... *172*
24. Creating Community via Classroom Discussions
by LeEdna Custer-Knight ... *181*
25. Working with Parents
by Joseph Sierzenga ... *189*
26. RTP and the School Bus Driver
by Rex C. Squires ... *198*
27. RTP in a Residential Setting on a Navajo Reservation
by Rod Bond ... *206*
28. The Coach's Corner
by Bill McCarrick ... *210*
29. A Janitor Sees All
by Bryan John Williams ... *218*
30. How I Became an RTP Trainer
by Tim Carey ... *219*
31. Perceptual Control Theory in the Classroom
by W. Thomas Bourbon ... *226*

A Personal Afterword ... *242*

Appendix 1. Responsible Thinking Process Card ... *244*
Appendix 2. Additional Resources ... *246*
Appendix 3. RTP Faculty Initial Assessment Form ... *247*
Appendix 4. Letter to Parents Announcing Program ... *248*

We hold these truths to be self-evident,
that all men are created equal,
that they are endowed by their Creator
with certain unalienable Rights,
that among these are Life, Liberty,
and the pursuit of Happiness.

Declaration of Independence

In Memory

Joseph T. Sierzenga III
1954–1997

On September 3, 1997, the first real tragedy struck our growing RTP family. Joe Sierzenga, the 43-year-old principal at Morrice Elementary School in Morrice, Michigan, was on his way to work when he was struck broadside by a driver who ran a stop sign. Joe died of injuries that evening.

I've had few really close friends in life. Joe was one of them. I met him at a workshop I was giving in 1991, where he became excited by my ideas on discipline in education and on PCT. Up until that time, he was one of many educators who were frustrated by what was happening in their field. Joe became an instant supporter of mine.

Joe was a man of very deep religious convictions, and he lived those convictions wherever he was. His prayer life and devotion to God held the highest priority in his life. Next was his family—his wife, Betsy, and their two children, Joseph and Jaimi. Finally, his students and faculty and, fortunately for me, his devotion to what I was doing and for me personally. We were kindred spirits in many ways: our faith, our families, and our devotion to children. We would spend hours on the phone working through ideas. His parting comment would often be, after discussing some ideas he'd come up with, "I'll fuss with those ideas some more and let you know."

He was one of those rare human beings who thought things through, offering many creative ideas for whatever was on the table. Yet he never asserted himself, always remaining quiet among his peers, thinking and reflecting, and his obvious humility was apparent to all. When he was asked, his deep understanding and well-thought-out ideas would come out of him naturally, in an unassuming way, as if they were so obvious. And he had a delightful sense of humor. He'd always refer to himself as "Ed's Polish connection." His bright smile and gentle manner hid the powerful thinker that he was.

His concern and love for children was unparalleled. Once, a student who frequently found himself in trouble had chosen to disrupt one too many times and had chosen to go home. The history of this child revealed rather extreme punishments by his parents, and there was genuine fear for this child. Joe decided that he would be the boy's parent. From that time, when the child was disrupting to the degree that a call to his father was needed, he would "go home to Joe's office" and talk with this "school Dad."

Joe is missed by all of us. He will be on my mind and in my prayers for as long as I live. He was a very special person. As Betsy said to me shortly after his death, "Ed, I've lost a best friend, and you've lost a best friend." She said it all.

To my grandchildren
Thomas Kane
Hester Kane
Georgietta Kuhn
Dorothy Kuhn
Eddie Ford
Ruth Ford
Sally Ann Ford
Nelson Johnson
Tess Ford
Hunter Johnson
Breen Ford
Christian Ford
Haley Ford
Brandt Ford
Lawson Ford
Patrick Ford
Emily Johnson
Preston Ford
and those who have not yet arrived ...

Acknowledgements

It has now been four years since the responsible thinking process (RTP) was begun at the Clarendon Elementary School in the Osborn School District in Phoenix. It is now in over 11 states and 50 schools, and, internationally, is in Germany and Australia. It is incredible how RTP has grown, but I certainly cannot take credit for all that has taken place.

George Venetis, who was administrative assistant at both Clarendon and Solano Elementary Schools and is now principal of Solano, and LeEdna Custer-Knight, school psychologist at Clarendon, are the first to be recognized. It was their belief in me as they helped me build RTP, and the Clarendon teachers' belief in them, that brought all of this about.

Darleen Martin, responsible thinking classroom (RTC) teacher at Clarendon, and Becky McNany, the teacher's aide who monitors the RTC, showed exceptional patience and devotion while we created this model.

I have a special spot in my heart for school secretaries. Barbara Redmond at Clarendon and Sherri Creer at Solano have been extremely supportive.

My thanks to John Champlin, a good friend and national authority on school restructuring, for writing the Introduction. I am indebted to Bill Powers, my friend and teacher, for writing the Foreword. He created the perceptual control theory (PCT) model, which is the basis of my work.

My thanks to Dag Forssell for his many suggestions.

Tom Bourbon, a close personal friend, is a research scientist who has created computer models demonstrating the scientific validity of PCT. In April 1996, he received a two-year grant to study my program, compare it to others, and develop some research. He's helped me build integrity and structure into RTP.

Tom's daughter, Caroline Young, has been his research assistant and created and edits *It's All Perception*, the RTP newsletter. A full-time special ed teacher, she spends her free time interviewing, writing, editing, and publishing. I really appreciate all she has done.

I'd like to thank all those who've written chapters for this revised edition. They've made the work of orchestrating the entire project much easier. You'll meet them and see what they've done in Part 2 of this book. There are many others, some mentioned in *Book Two*, who have been of great support. Steve Smith, principal of the Boyne City Middle School, a supporter of RTP since it began, is the first to come to mind. So is Phil Homer, superintendent of Blaine County School District in Hailey, Idaho, along with Jim Lewis, his assistant superintendent; Tom Turos, superintendent of the Catalina Mt. School in Tucson, a lockup facility of the Arizona Department of Juvenile Corrections, Alan Mielke, principal of the school, and Sonia Vernon, assistant principal; Jim Sandoval, principal, and Chris Eaton, RTC teacher, Maryvale High School, Phoenix Union High School District; Jodi Bernhardt, assistant principal, and Laurie King, RTC teacher, Heatherbrae Elementary School, Cartwright School District, Phoenix; Jack Foster, lead teacher, and Ted Huerta, RTC teacher, Casa Blanca Community School, Gila River Indian Reservation, Bapchule, Arizona; Bobbi McClernan, RTC teacher at the elementary school, Mayer Unified School District, Mayer, Arizona; Nola Johnson, RTC teacher at Solano; Mark Yslas, assistant principal, and Briley Culton, RTC teacher, Squaw Peak Elementary School, Creighton Elementary School District, Phoenix; Don Nelson, middle school principal, Page Unified School District, Page, Arizona; Mike Helminski, principal, Kiva Elementary School, Scottsdale Unified School District, Scottsdale, Arizona; Sam Vidulich, director of elementary and family faith, Blessed Sacrament Church, Phoenix; and Jake Jacobs, a close friend and probation officer with the Maricopa County Adult Probation Department, who has helped me extend this work to probation.

Overseas, Tim Carey has done an enormous amount of work in Australia. He personally worked to get Tom and I to the land "down under," and then, at his own expense, spent three weeks in the U.S. studying the process. Stefan Balke, Bielefeld, Germany, has attempted to implement RTP via e-mail. Finally, a big thanks to Margaret Brown, who created the artwork on RTP and PCT. A behavior intervention specialist with the Queensland education department in Australia, she has been an active supporter of my program.

My thanks to my son-in-law, Eric Johnson, who created my web page (`http://www.respthink.com/`) and my respthink net, while keeping me functioning with my computer. I'm especially appreciative of my brother, Tom, and his wife, Susan, for their confidence in RTP and support that has helped me build the needed integrity and structure into the program. My thanks also to my sister, Amy Weden, a retired middle school teacher. As my editor, she insisted that I write clearly and think logically. And a special thanks to Greg Williams, my final editor, typesetter, and more importantly, advisor. He is also the archivist for the Control Systems Group, the organization for those who study and research PCT.

Finally, thank you, Hester. After 47 years of marriage, eight children, and an increasing number of grandchildren, our love grows daily. With the Grace of God, it will continue.

Edward E. Ford, M.S.W.
Phoenix, Arizona
November 18, 1997

Introduction

It has been interesting to watch education and educators confront the issue of inappropriate behavior. The problem is not one restricted to student discipline. Teaching staffs frequently find themselves at odds in the place where they work. The result is behaviors that are not satisfying to anyone. It is not especially startling to reflect that the place in which we live and work is not a sufficiently satisfying place. My personal quest is to redesign and reshape the internal functioning of schools so that discipline is no longer a significant issue. We will create places that are at the same time challenging, needs fulfilling, and meaningful. There will be no need for negative behaviors.

Perceptual control theory promises to be a major instrument in this quest. We are finally challenging the industrial factory model. Control and coercion serve only to contain and restrict. It is time that we stop being in charge of people and afford each person the challenge and the opportunity to be personally responsible for their behaviors and the decisions which influence their daily living.

We are on the verge of significant paradigm shifts. Perceptual control theory will be our catalyst.

Ed Ford has done an exceptional job in creating a very workable process to confront the need for students to make appropriate, responsible choices. It is in these challenges that we can finally connect people, choices, responsibility, and accountability. Ed's work is thoughtful, scholarly, and provocative. In our work of redesigning schools, perceptual control theory has become our chief resource for developing responsible behaviors. Be it student or adult, we are finally getting to focus our energies through a process which helps us to identify positive and contributing behaviors and to screen out those that are non-contributing. We no longer have to suffer through actions and attitudes that we formerly found difficult if not impossible to manage.

John Champlin
Scottsdale, Arizona
May 5, 1994

Foreword

If you just listen to the words used in this book, you might get an uncomfortable feeling about Ed Ford's recommendations and insights. Discipline, establishing rules, obedience, making commitments, responsibility—to anyone who has gone through conventional school systems as a student, these words have a familiar and threatening ring: they mean *shape up!*

But you will do well to hear more than just these words. Behind them is a theory called *perceptual control theory*, or PCT, but even more important, behind them is Ed Ford and many years of experience dealing successfully with people who have problems. New psychological theories promise radical changes in the way people deal with each other, particularly with problems between people. In the hands of ivory-tower academics or fanatics, they can quickly lead to disaster. The reason is the very newness of the theories, newness that means the need for a long period of testing and correcting before errors have been found and removed. The only real test for a theory about human nature is in the real world, where conditions are not controlled and the "experimental subjects" have no idea how they are supposed to behave, except what their own natures tell them. That is the world of Ed Ford, and the world in which he is applying—with a strong sense of the possible—the principles of perceptual control theory.

The real trick in applying a new theory like PCT to real people in real situations is to know what is possible to change and what is better left the way it is until we know more. The changes that Ed outlines in this book are all possible to make. Ed has shown people how to make them, and where they have been put into effect, the results have been enthusiastically received. Yet there are few radical changes here; the effects of the theory are seen mostly as shifts in attitude, changes in the kind of respect that people show for each other, a lessening of coercion and control that naturally occurs as human nature itself becomes better understood.

Paradoxically, perceptual "control" theory is not about how to control people better; it is about the inborn nature of human beings as independent organisms who control themselves, who are inherently in charge of what happens to themselves. This view of human nature is quite different from traditional ideas still influential in society, which teach that human behavior is caused by everything *but* the person doing the behaving. A word like "discipline" takes on an entirely new meaning when you start from the premise that only the individual can exert discipline—that is, use internal principles and rules as a guide for living. This is not one person trying to force another into behaving right. It is an individual trying to make personal sense of standards, goals, and relationships with other people. Achieving discipline in the classroom is no longer a question of cowing children into sitting quietly in rows; it is a question of communicating to children their own power to make choices and decisions, to pick workable goals and achieve them, to find a reasonable and pleasant way to live with others—who are also independent, self-disciplined beings.

The implications of PCT in terms of self-understanding and understanding society are potentially immense. But they are also largely unexplored. It would be very easy to jump to extreme conclusions, to interpret the meaning of PCT as supporting either a stodgy status quo or a radical descent into license and anarchy. This is why Ed Ford's approach is so important. In any part of our society, there is already a social system in place, with its rules and customs, its institutions and laws. It is there because it works —maybe not always very well, maybe not to everyone's benefit, but certainly better than nature red in tooth and claw. Ed Ford knows very well where we are, and that to get anywhere else we must start here.

When we tinker with this system, we know not what we do. A new theory is no excuse for taking an axe to the whole structure of the school system, or the social system in general. What must be done is to look for the aspects of the system that clearly need change, and that clearly can be changed without destroying everything. The insights of PCT can be applied non-destructively to key human relationships that are not working the way we want them to work. We can leave everything else the way it is—until we understand what to do next.

This is how Ed Ford works. In this book you will find many conventional ideas and methods, but every time Ed speaks of them, you will see that they are approached from a new direction, with a new attitude that makes all the difference. Pay attention to the difference; it is what makes this approach both effective and practical.

William T. Powers
Durango, Colorado
April 24, 1994

A Word of Caution about
Starting the Program

Many teachers who have attempted to use the responsible thinking process (RTP) program tend to perceive its questioning protocol as just another means for controlling students. Nothing could be further from the truth. This mistake is possible only without an understanding of perceptual control theory (PCT), upon which RTP is based. Children are autonomous human beings who should be treated with respect. Those who believe that they can control children, either by conditioning them with rewards and punishments or by meeting all of their "needs," cannot make this program work. If the RTP questions are asked in a quiet, curious, respectful tone, and if the student is willing to deal with the questions, then the questions act as a teaching guide by which the student, pondering the answers, learns to think through the conflicts with which he is dealing. He also perceives the teachers as non-critical and non-controlling. As he considers the unintended consequences of his actions, he learns to make plans such that, whatever choices he makes, his actions carry with them the intent to respect the rights of others.

The person who is responsible for administering the program needs more than just an understanding that children are autonomous. This administrator must be willing to make the necessary efforts to deal with those who are critical of the program, to protect the program's funding, to deal with political issues, and to deal with a district office, parents, and faculty members who lack commitment or understanding of what the program is all about. Not only must she deal with those teachers who refuse to use the program by holding them accountable for student disruption, but also *she must never permit those teachers to corrupt the use of the responsible thinking classroom (RTC) by using it as a detention center*. They should never be permitted to send students to the RTC unless they use the process. Finally, the administrator should also deal quickly and decisively with those students who choose to leave the RTC by disrupting.

If you are seriously considering the RTP program, you must find out whether the faculty members are satisfied with their present program. A sample faculty survey form to be used for that purpose is shown in Appendix 3. If most of the faculty are satisfied with the present program, it would be difficult or impossible to introduce a new program, especially one that requires teachers to change the way they deal with students. If the faculty is not satisfied, then usually a core group of teachers, parents, and administrators representing the school, often called a discipline committee, should read both of my books on school discipline, this book and *Discipline for Home and School, Book Two: Program Standards for Schools*. They should also view the video on the program produced by a Phoenix TV station and "The Heart of the Process" video. If the committee finds RTP acceptable, they should purchase copies of this book for everyone on the staff, and copies of *Book Two* for the professional staff. Those interested in learning more about PCT and its theoretical models, upon which this program is based, should read my book *Freedom From Stress*.

If, after having read the books and viewed the videos, at least 75% of the professional staff commit to the program, then the staff will need training *from a person who is presently certified as a trainer by Ed Ford & Associates. A certified administrator is not qualified to do this training*. I recommend one or two days of training, with a follow-up day several months later. Questions and concerns of the staff, along with added training, make up the agenda of the follow-up day. If a second initial day is requested, it could be used to provide more staff training on the questioning techniques and plan making, as well as time with the responsible thinking classroom (RTC) teacher and the RTP administrator, going over the use of forms and suggesting the layout of the room. Prior to initiating the program, a letter should be sent home to parents, explaining the new discipline program. See Appendix 4.

Finally, the ideal way to begin RTP is with district office support. Because RTP is so different, both in theory and in practice, from what is being done in most schools, it would be extremely helpful to have the full administrative backing of the central office.

As George Venetis, principal of a school using RTP, wisely observed, many educators think that RTP will eliminate all school discipline problems, but it won't. They're looking for that magic program that will cure disrupting students, but it doesn't exist. The struggle to take responsibility for their lives must take place within students; they must learn to reorganize their way of thinking. And this takes time. Thus, students must be given the needed time and on-going support to deal with their conflicts. RTP provides the most effective way for teaching students to be responsible while maintaining a non-punitive, respectful relationship with them as they learn to take responsibility for their lives.

In order to protect the integrity of the program, Ed Ford & Associates will offer recognition to those schools that are successfully using the responsible thinking process. This recognition, in the form of certification, is given when the RTP administrator has demonstrated a good understanding of PCT, the RTP administrator and the RTC teacher are both performing their roles, a majority of teachers are using the process, and appropriate data have been kept for one year.

The cost for materials can be found inside the back cover of this book. To make arrangements for training, contact Ed Ford & Associates, 10209 N. 56th St., Scottsdale, AZ 85253, phone 602-991-4860. For the latest information on RTP, including any price changes and additional materials, visit our Web site: `http://www.respthink.com/`.

Part 1. The Basics of RTP

Chapter 1
What This Book Is All About

In recent years, I have spent much time working with parents, teachers, counselors, and school administrators across the United States. I have found in school after school and home after home that there is a desperate need for an efficient and workable discipline program. The reason is obvious. Children are growing up without the social skills they need. Many of them lack the ability to cooperate with their parents, teachers, and peers. They haven't learned to obey rules. And they haven't learned to discipline *themselves*—this means setting their own rules and standards, setting measurable and objective goals, and creating for themselves an orderly way of life so that they can accomplish their own goals in an efficient way. To achieve this, they must first learn through experience to obey the established rules and standards of the environments in which they find themselves every day.

This requires something new: help with social skills for children who have the need and are willing to learn, teaching them how to respect the rights of others, how to get along with their peers, how to make effective plans for studying and self-discipline, how to understand the purpose of rules, and how to work with adults in a cooperative atmosphere. In short, teaching children *responsible thinking*.

The reasons for the rise in disruptive behavior at home and in schools are fairly obvious. Excessive television has deprived children of the time in which they most naturally develop, through play activity, the social skills that they need for getting along with others. It is in creative play that they learn how to set limits, negotiate, compromise, and respect each others' rights. And in the school years, much of their after-school play time is regulated and controlled, with rules set and supervision established by their parents or coaches. *They haven't spent enough time learning how to get along with others through play on their own*. It is rare today to see children organizing themselves in activities in which they can develop an ability to get along with others and learn respect for the rights of others.

The fact that children have to *learn* the skills of getting along with others implies the need for some creative thinking on their part. This kind of thinking is rarely taught. Instead, children are treated with drugs, manipulated, punished, or subjected to other forms of intervention. In most cases, adults decide what happens to them.

A number of years ago, I worked as a consultant at the Adobe Mountain Juvenile Correction Facility just north of Phoenix, one of Arizona's maximum security facilities for juveniles. My job was to train case managers and security officers how to deal with the young offenders. I was assigned to two units. In one unit, no one was really interested in what I had to offer. In the other unit, I found one officer and one case manager who wanted to learn from me. So I went to the superintendent and suggested several alternatives: he could cancel my contract, I could work on a limited basis, or I could look for case managers in other units at the facility who might be interested in what I had to offer. He insisted that I stay and look for interested staff. I found some. I offered some general workshops for the entire staff at the facility, and then I started working directly with the juveniles in the units, with the counselors and officers watching how I interacted with their charges.

I found that, to a person, when I asked the juveniles what they wanted to work on that would help them get out of lock-up, their inability to control their anger was their major concern. I would ask them what happened the last time they got upset, and invariably they would say that they had "punched someone out." I would ask, "Is there anyone you know who does something different?" "Yeah," they would reply, "Thomas goes to his room when he gets upset." "And what does he do there?" "He writes poems." "What do you think of how he handles his anger?" "Well, he doesn't go to lock-up, and he'll get out of here quicker than I will," came the reply. I taught them how to work out plans for themselves to help deal more effectively with their anger. Some chose to go to their cells and read when upset, others chose to sleep, and still others chose to do push-ups. One young man dealt with his anger problem by "taking a mile-and-a-half walk" in his cell (his cell was 10 feet wide; he walked back-and-forth across it enough times to cover a mile and a half). He said that by walking, he became calm again.

Before I arrived, teaching responsible thinking was rarely attempted with these juveniles. When I attended diagnostic meetings at the facility, the personnel sat around discussing an offender's record and what they thought ought to be "done" with him. During staff meetings, where the juvenile was confronted by those who dealt with him on a daily basis, often he was verbally attacked and criticized; when he would try to defend himself, they would often ignore him. In schools and at home, I've often found the same thing. Children are tested, put on various types of medication, diagnosed, sent to various types of groups and programs, and classified, but only rarely are they taught to think things through on their own, to deal with what they see as important to them—what *they* want to work on.

Children are suspended in-school and "grounded" at home, they are given detention, they are lectured to, and they are yelled at and criticized—all of this supposedly to produce children who think creatively and responsibly about how they should handle themselves when faced with social problems. But the only thing that these kinds of punishment teach children is how to punish. And so students get back at the system through vandalism and disruption and acting out. Only rarely does anyone sit down and find out from children whether they want to work at making their lives better.

In this book, I have put together some ideas on discipline that have *worked* in the schools and with families where they have been tried. That doesn't mean that what I have written about cannot be improved. I hope that others will build upon what I have suggested here. Some schools where I have worked have already done so, adding practical applications of their own (see Part 2). No one has all the answers. We are all trying to help each other in a very difficult task.

My program is based on the work of William T. Powers, whose perceptual control theory (PCT) models have been amply documented in the scientific literature (see references in Chapter 31). PCT offers a completely new approach to discipline. Asking children what they want, how they perceive things, and whether what they're doing is helping them to achieve all of their goals, then offering them choices are the steps to treating children as living control systems about whom we care and in whom we believe —living control systems who must learn to think and act responsibly when interacting with other living control systems in order to be able to achieve their own goals.

Perceptual control theory teaches that all humans are trying to achieve their own internally specified goals; they do so by acting on the world so that their perceptions are what they want them to be. This is not done in a vacuum—it is done mostly around others. If, while attempting to control my own perceptual world, I limit someone else from doing the same thing, then I violate the rights of another human being.

Trying to teach children (as living control systems) to control their own perceptions without interfering with the rights of other living control systems to do the same is sometimes viewed as trying to control the children. But there is a big difference between trying to control what happens to another person and asking that person what choice they prefer among the options they currently have. It is respecting their right to control their own destiny that makes the difference.

It is essential that children be given the choice *when they are ready to reconcile their problems, not when parents or teachers think they are ready*. If a child is sent to a restricted area and then is not allowed to be reconciled when she is ready, providing that her teacher or parent is free at that moment to deal with her, then the restriction could be perceived by her as punitive, since she is ready and no one wants to talk with her. If she is asked to reconcile before she is ready to accept responsibility, then she will most likely become disruptive again and develop a sense of failure, since she has not yet made any commitment to resolve her problems. The child needs to be allowed to control her destiny within the reality of the environment in which she finds herself. That will allow her the maximum opportunity to learn to control her own world.

The more understanding parents and school personnel have of how we all think, act, and function as living control systems, the greater are the chances for children to succeed, that is, to achieve their own goals in ways that do not interfere with the success of others. So I begin with an introduction to perceptual control theory.

Chapter 2
A Simple Understanding
of Perceptual Control Theory

Every sound program needs an equally sound theoretical basis. For this program, perceptual control theory (PCT) is the basis. PCT was developed by William T. Powers and researched by members of the Control Systems Group (see Appendix 2). This chapter provides an overview of PCT, using a story to illustrate the basic ideas.

Hunter wasn't Mrs. Johnson's favorite fourth grade student. He had been in trouble for most of the week, getting out of his seat and wandering around the classroom, talking when she was trying to teach the class, and constantly borrowing pencils and paper.

Today, Hunter was supposed to be working on his spelling. He didn't want to do his spelling—he wanted some attention. Sally Ann, who was busy doing her work, sat across the aisle from Hunter. He thought she was cute, and he liked her happy smile. He wanted her to notice him.

"Sally Ann, psst! Hi!" She looked over, smiled and giggled, then looked down at her paper. For a short time, Hunter had gotten what he wanted. He perceived Sally Ann's smile and giggle as signs of affection and caring. He wanted the pleasure to continue. Again, he tried to get Sally Ann's attention. "Psst, Sally Ann, hi!"

This second attempt at getting Sally Ann's attention did not go unnoticed by Mrs. Johnson. She looked at Hunter and said, "Hunter, please stop talking." Hunter looked up and said nothing. Then he pretended to return to his spelling exercise, while writing a note to Sally Ann.

What did Hunter *want*? He wanted to perceive Sally Ann

caring about him and paying attention to him. And what did Hunter *perceive*? He perceived Sally Ann as working at her desk, ignoring him, not caring about him. Hunter compared what he wanted with his perception and found that there was a big *difference* between his goal and his perception. That difference caused him a lot of pain.

Now, how do you suppose Hunter tried to get rid of the pain which was caused by the difference between wanting Sally Ann to notice him and what he saw, which was Sally Ann busily doing her school work? Obviously, he tried to get her attention by making noise and calling her name.

What do you think was *most* on Mrs. Johnson's mind? What was she thinking about at the time Hunter called to Sally Ann? Think about your own life and how you handle things. Suppose one of your own children is yelling at another child; what are the dominant concerns in your mind? They probably are that you want to experience quiet in the house.

Imagine being Hunter's teacher, trying to maintain quiet in her class, so the children could focus on their work, and so she could be free to help those who seemed to need it, while Hunter was trying to get a little girl's attention. What is the first thing that would come to your mind? Obviously, you would want Hunter to do his work and not disturb other children.

The point is that *what comes to our minds is what we want*. The reason it comes to our minds is that we perceive something which does not compare favorably to what we want. In the case of a parent, it could be yelling and screaming replacing the calm in the house. To a teacher, it could be talking in the classroom. If I were walking down the street with my wife, Hester, and a car were to drive by at what I consider to be a reasonable speed, I'd probably not give the car's passing a second thought. But if it were to drive by at 80 miles per hour, that would conflict with my own internal goal of what a safe speed should be.

The only time we have concerns is when we have a perception which is contrary to our goals. It is comparing what we perceive around us to what we want that drives us to *change our actions*, but *only* when there are differences between the two. If everything compares favorably, then we don't have any concerns, and we don't change what we are doing. Thus, in Hunter's case, what drives his actions is the difference between his goal and what he sees Sally Ann doing.

Human beings act when they are trying to *control* their perception of the world to make it conform to internally set goals. But many things in the world that affect our perceptions keep changing or varying. Thus, people try to control their perceptions by acting on those things that affect their perceptions. In Hunter's case, he acted by making the noise "Psst." The diagrams below show Hunter's control system in operation.

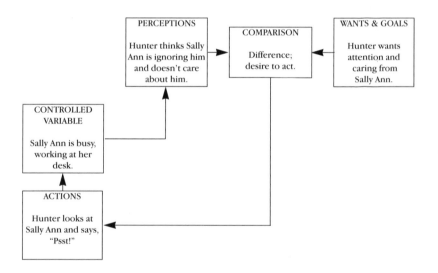

And it *worked*. As the next diagram shows, Sally Ann looked at Hunter, smiled, and giggled. *Hunter was satisfied* because he perceived Sally Ann as caring, whether she did or not.

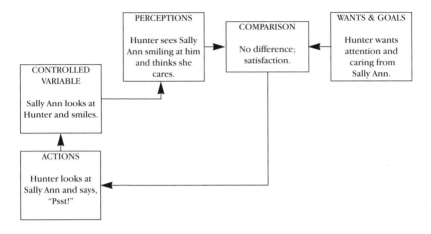

But it worked only *temporarily*. Sally Ann soon stopped paying attention to Hunter, and again there was a difference between his goal and his perception. So Hunter again acted on the outside world to make his perceptions conform to his goal. This time, however, something else happened. Mrs. Johnson, the teacher, disapproved of Hunter's actions. She said to Hunter, "Hunter, please stop talking." Hunter said nothing and pretended to go back to work. In Hunter's world, Mrs. Johnson was a *disturbance* affecting

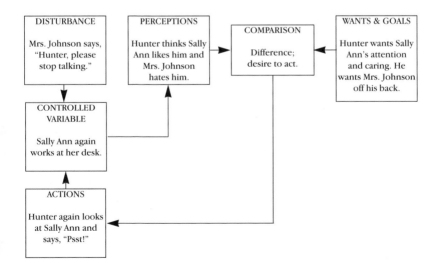

his attempt to control his perception of the way he wanted Sally Ann to be.

Hunter was afraid to continue saying "Psst!" to try to get Sally Ann's attention. He now had to look busy to get around Mrs. Johnson's concern for noise. But there was still a difference between his desire for Sally Ann's attention and his perception of Sally Ann. So he tried an *alternative* action in an attempt to *get around* the effect of the disturbance (Mrs. Johnson) and to achieve his primary goal of getting Sally Ann's attention. Hunter sent Sally Ann a note.

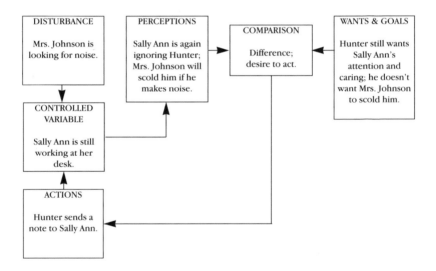

Guess what—it worked! Sally Ann looked at Hunter, smiled again, and Hunter was again satisfied. This movement produced no noise, and Mrs. Johnson, who wanted quiet in her room, was satisfied that the noise had stopped. And it had. Hunter had evaded the disturbance and had gotten what he wanted. The point here is that our perceptions don't always match the real world. Sally Ann might not have cared for Hunter, and though it was quiet, not all of the students were necessarily studying.

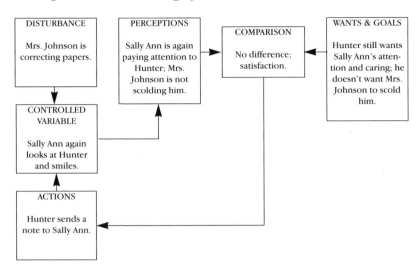

The above illustrates the basic ideas of perceptual control theory. We always act to control our perceptions. We're always comparing the way we want things to be with the way we perceive them to be. If what we perceive is the same as what we want, then we are satisfied. If what we perceive is not the same as what we want, then we try to eliminate the difference by changing what we want or by acting on the world to change what we perceive. *The details of how we perform the actions are of little importance to us. Getting our perceptions to conform to what we want is our major concern.* Our environment is filled with other people and natural forces, which often keep our perceptions of the world from conforming to what we want. We act in *whatever ways are necessary* to eliminate or cancel the effects of those disturbances on our perceptions which we are trying to control.

If you are interested in learning more about the ideas of perceptual control theory and how they relate to RTP, I recommend that you read Chapter 31.

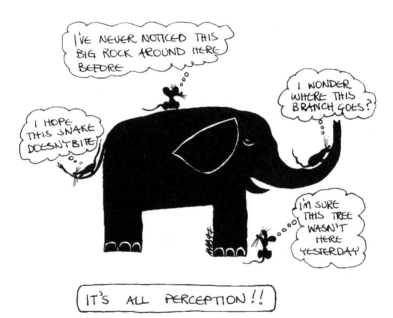

Chapter 3
What Is Discipline?

Discipline is teaching children to respect the rights of others through responsible thinking by learning to obey rules. The key word is *think*. It was his thinking that got Hunter into trouble. His actions merely reflected his thoughts in his attempts to get Sally Ann to notice him. Thus, discipline begins and ends with teaching children to think out the soundness of what they want, relative to how they presently perceive what they are getting and to how they are attempting to accomplish their goal as it relates to the rules and standards of wherever they are and to the rights of others. In terms of PCT, it means teaching children to control their perceptions while trying to reduce, as much as possible, disturbing others.

Most school programs are designed to control the actions of children, with very little thinking involved. Their names are put on the board, they are told to sit in the corner for a specific amount of time, and they are often yelled at or criticized. When a teacher's efforts fail, most educators give children detention or suspension for a specific amount of time from school, and they assume that when children return to class or school, somehow they will have learned to obey the rules. This rarely works!

PCT says, loudly and clearly, that *you can't control another person's behavior*. Trying to control children by rewarding or punishing them does not teach responsible thinking—it teaches children to manipulate others and to "con" the system. Trying to control children also does another thing. It irritates them. And the more children are irritated, the more angry they get, leading to chaos.

There is simply no way anyone is going to control children except in major lock-up facilities—and even there, they are very difficult to deal with! PCT says that *people are designed to control their own perceptions*. The only way to develop *self*-disciplined children is by teaching them to think responsibly for themselves, which means to control their own perceptions without disturbing others. And the only way for adults to help children do this is by asking questions.

To some, giving children limited choices appears to be a form of punishment. I define punishment as trying to change what children do by hurting them, either physically or verbally, or giving them no options or choices. With discipline, none of the options might be what a child currently wants, but there are no other options available to the person in charge of the child.

The ideal home or school is one where children are happy and safe, where there is no vandalism, and where children can learn and play without disruption. This is a home or school where children have been given opportunities to learn the necessary social skills so that they can think and act responsibly. This is what a good discipline program should provide.

Chapter 4
When Should Discipline Be Used?

In general, children are given progressively more freedom according to their ability to handle the privileges that they enjoy. For example, as babies grow, their parents allow them greater freedom to roam the house, use the kitchen, and play with others unsupervised. And in the schools, teachers and administrators expect more responsibility from sixth graders than from children in kindergarten.

In a discipline program, the more children can demonstrate their ability and willingness to act appropriately in social situations, the more privileges they can be given. At the heart of such maturity is respect for the rights of those with whom they interact, whether at school, at home, or elsewhere in the community. Wherever people live together, all need to respect the rights of others by following established rules and standards.

For instance, in the classroom, teachers have the right to teach, and students have the right to learn. When children act in ways that keep teachers from teaching and that keep other children from learning, or in ways that bring harm to themselves or others, there is a discipline problem. Children have no more right to disrupt a classroom than adults do to disrupt a courtroom, an employee meeting at work, or a dinner party at a restaurant. Any type of disruption that acts as a disturbance to others who are trying to achieve their own goals constitutes a violation of the rights of others.

But some actions, although undesirable, are not discipline problems that disturb others. Students who fail to finish their homework or forget to bring a pencil, paper, or book to class are not causing a disruption. Some teachers or supervisors send children out of class for failing to do an assignment, inadvertently or accidentally dropping something on the floor, or daydreaming, but these actions really have little to do with class disruptions. Such matters do not require giving social skills training to the children involved. Social skills training *is* required when, for example, a student bothers another while the latter is trying to study, or when a student pushes, shoves, or trips another student, or when children speak out when another student is talking, or when children come into class late, or when children throw things during class—namely, when children try to attract attention and distract other children who are studying or listening to the instructions of the teacher.

The same is true at home. Children have no right to take what belongs to their parents or siblings, no right to make fun of others, and no right to interrupt conversations. Parents and their children have a right to demand that their home be a safe environment where everyone is treated with respect.

Discipline should always be tied to lack of respect for others: the uninvited intrusion into another's activities or private concerns; the unnecessary disturbance of another person's attempts to control his own perceptions. It simply comes down to the violation of another person's rights.

Chapter 5
Establishing Discipline

Unless coaches know what they are doing and work closely together, their team isn't going to win any games. Nothing could be more true when it comes to discipline at home and in school. Parents who fight and argue and, at the same time, expect to have a disciplined house are going to be very disappointed. They need to work well together so that their children will learn by example and experience how to respect the rights of others. If parents don't show respect for each other, how are children to learn what respecting the rights of others is all about?

Thus, parents should have strong relationships with each other, as well as with their children. From observing their parents' relationship, children learn what a satisfying relationship is all about. And they also learn through the example of their parents that only by working together do people succeed in their mutual goals. First, parents should have an agreed-to strategy for raising their children, especially when it comes to establishing the rules and standards of the home. In this kind of atmosphere, children experience the harmony that comes from a well-organized home. They know what to expect from their parents. Parents should be both fair and consistent in the treatment of their children. More importantly, parents should be aware that for children to have their rights respected as well as to learn to respect the rights of others, those rights have to be defined by the rules and standards of the home. Thus, specifically established rules allow the children to gain responsibility in a secure environment.

In school, it is critical that teachers, counselors, and

administrators work together to develop and implement the standards and rules of the school. LeEdna Custer-Knight, the school psychologist at Clarendon Elementary School in the Osborn School District in Phoenix, says that the critical requirement for establishing a discipline program is not only a total commitment of the staff, but a strong *core team* of teachers, parents, and administrators, representing school personnel plus the community, all of whom constantly work together to solve the problems that continually arise. "There has to be an agreed-to understanding of the strategy for handling students and a consistency in what we do. It's a slow process to implement this, but with a total commitment on the part of everyone, and especially the staff, it can be done."

In order for a group of people to succeed *they must continually align their goals and how they perceive what they're trying to change with other members of their team.* An administrator cannot work in isolation from the school staff, nor can counselors work without parents, nor can children improve their lives without being part of the problem-solving process. Everyone has to work cooperatively, or conflict will reign.

At the same time, children have to learn to live with the different personalities of the key adults in their world. Parents might agree about the rules in the home, but as individuals they might disagree as to how to apply particular rules. The same is true at school. The way children are treated is bound to vary from classroom to classroom and within the other settings in which children find themselves. But rather than confuse children, these differences merely prepare them for life. Certainly their friends are all different, as are the homes in which their friends live. Later, in their work life, they will find that their various customers each have different standards, as do their various supervisors and peers.

Finally, any core team in a school should include a key member of the school staff, namely the school secretary. In most schools, no one is better at sensing the pulse of a school and how it is doing than this person. Secretaries deal with the constant flow of parents and children through the office, handling the endless stream of complaints and concerns, some of which they deal with and some of which they channel to the appropriate persons.

The core team concept tends to handle problems in a more efficient way, while keeping the rest of the staff updated on their various decisions. Any method that creates a more effective operation means that children have a better chance of learning in a safe environment. In short, the school or home that works efficiently together, stays together. Those who work separately remain in chaos.

Chapter 6
When Are Children
Willing to Learn Discipline?

Whenever someone is having problems with a child, re-gardless of the circumstances, the first question that should be asked is how much *quality time* those who are impor-tant to the child have been spending with him. Anyone's ability to resolve problems, to stand firm in the face of adversity, and to work through difficult conflicts depends on the strength that comes from personal relationships out of which develops a strong belief in self. Disruption and act-ing-out are symptomatic of a fundamental problem: in-security fed by the loneliness that comes from a lack of warm, caring, joyful relationships.

From my experience in working with families and con-sulting in schools, corrections, mental health, and resi-dential treatment centers over many years, plus raising my own eight children, I believe that nothing is more impor-tant than our individual alone time with our spouse and with each of our children. Children create their percep-tions of their parents based on the time they have spent with them and the *quality* of that time. We all tend to listen to and respect those whom we perceive respect us, who care about us, and have expressed, both verbally and by their actions, a belief that we have worth as a human being.

What gives a teacher or parent true access to children is when the children believe that whoever is working with them cares about them and, more importantly, believes in their ability to resolve their problems. If you don't have confidence in your children's ability to succeed, they'll know it, and that lack of belief will very likely translate into your children's lack of confidence in themselves. Thus, the most important step when teaching responsible thinking involves spending the kind of time that is going to create this belief on the part of children that someone cares about them. I call this *quality time*. This is discussed in detail in my books *Love Guaranteed* and *Freedom From Stress*.

With this belief in themselves, children are able to commit to themselves not only a promise to resolve their problems, but also to do so *cooperatively with those who spend individual alone time with them*. Over the past 30 years, I have taught couples and parents with children how to build sufficient strength in their marriages and families so that they could resolve their problems in reasonable and rational ways. Quality time is the only effective program I've found that will create the kind of love and trust needed for relationships to survive and grow.

From perceptual control theory, I have learned that we create our perception of others from mutual, interactive types of experiences that people have with each other. The criteria for these experiences are as follows: first, whatever you do, you must be *aware* of each other; second, you must create the enjoyment, rather than passively watch TV or a movie; third, you must spend this time *alone together* with whomever you are trying to build a relationship; and fourth, this activity should happen on a *daily or regular basis*.

The success stories using quality time are many. I once had a single parent tell me that she had never had a day's problem with her 18-year-old son. The boy's father had left her prior to her son's birth. She said to me, "When my son first began to walk, I resolved right then that he and I would take a walk every day of our lives together." And she added, "We've done that. Many times he'd come home from school and he'd say to me, 'Come on, Mom, we gotta take our walk.'"

The greatest story of all was during a group meeting with former prison inmates, on probation. I was running these groups for Jake Jacobs, an adult probation officer. I had asked the group members what were the toughest problems they had on probation. Most talked about disagreements with their spouses or live-in friends. One man whom I will call Charlie said that he had been doing well with his girlfriend for the past three months. When I asked what he was doing, he said, "We take a long walk every night." I asked how he figured this out. He pointed to Jake and said, "He gave me this card on quality time. It said you had to take a walk, and that's what I've been doing." Charlie had been a drug addict since he was eight years old. He was then 38 and had been a recovering addict for two years. He'd been in and out of prison many times, gone through two marriages, and had, in succession, lived with and beaten up 15 to 20 women. A year after he told me this, he was still succeeding with his girlfriend. He invited Jake and myself to his wedding but had to delay it because he wanted his son, who was in prison, to be best man. Today, Charlie is married, is still taking his walks, and is still doing well.

Over the years, as I was developing my ideas on quality time, I never realized that the best example was right under my own nose. I'm speaking of my lovely wife, Hester. It was only after our grandchildren began to appear that I became conscious of how she really worked with children. As they would arrive at our home for a visit or an overnight stay, no sooner would they be in the door than she would be down on the floor with them, doing a puzzle, coloring a picture, playing a card game, or figuring out the rules of a board game. Or she would be off on a bike ride, or taking a walk down the street, or having a tea party, or creating something in the kitchen. She takes children to her poster shop, and there they answer the phone, or help my son, Thomas, who runs the framing department. Hester set up an area in her store for children, with a small table and chair, and with blocks and other creative toys with which they can play while their parents are shopping around. Often, when their parents want to leave, the children want to stay and play.

For outings, Hester takes children to the train park, or to the zoo, or to one of the local art museums, or to climb one of the many mountains around Phoenix. My daughter

Dorothy does the same with her two children. The rest of the family claims that she's the only mother who is going to wear out her children! She's always on the move, and she and her husband, Eric, constantly expose their children to the many experiences that can enhance a child's world.

Thus, the key to raising children has to do with *creating an atmosphere* in which youngsters are likely to obey rules and to learn to think responsibly, and their parents, in turn, have access to working with them. Quality time is the only kind of activity that will create that kind of atmosphere. This also means that not only must parents set rules and standards that reflect the parents' own values and beliefs, but they must follow through with the natural restrictions that flow from refusal to follow rules. In turn, all children eventually must learn to respect the rules of the culture in which they live, or they will be in conflict with the people in that culture. My experience with my own children has taught me that children tend to adopt the standards and values of their parents *if they've established a close, loving relationship with them, and if the choices they have made that reflect those values and standards in the home have brought them a satisfying life*. Ultimately, if children perceive you as caring about them, as believing in them, and if they recognize the existence of reasonable standards within the home, they are more likely to work cooperatively to find a way to get along.

For teachers and administrators, spending time with children individually at school can, at best, be limited to only a few children per adult. For some counselors, it might be easier, but in many schools where the paper work and the constant demand of students is high, counselors can be overwhelmed. Probably the single most effective way for teachers, administrators, and counselors to build some rapport with their children, while at the same time teaching them social skills, is by gathering the children together, seating them in a full circle of chairs (ever try talking with others with their backs to you?), and engaging them in discussions. It is in such settings that children can be efficiently taught by experience to listen and respect what their peers and teachers say. As they learn to respect the thoughts and opinions of the other students by watching the example of their teachers, they learn to respect the children and teachers themselves. The teacher's job is to make sure that no one is criticized or made fun of, in short, to maintain a fair and non-critical climate. When the more timid students see that it's safe to speak, they will enter into the class discussions. As the facilitator, the teacher makes no judgments about what is being said but, through questioning in a non-critical way, stimulates thinking. As perceptual control theory teaches, the way to access another's world is by asking questions. Thus, the best way to get a discussion going is by asking questions that relate to something of interest to the children. I find that it helps to ask children questions with some connection to their own personal experiences, so that they can respond from their own perceptions of life. Other questions could involve solving either real or fictional class problems.

My late friend Joe Sierzenga, elementary principal at Morrice Elementary School in Morrice, Michigan, told me about an incident in which he used this discussion technique with some of his students as a tool to teach them how to resolve a conflict with which they were trying to deal. A number of the boys had been hurt playing soccer, and he was asked to help them resolve their problem. First, he got them into a circle and asked them what they saw as the problem. When they told him that they were getting hurt playing soccer, he asked them what they wanted. "To play without getting hurt." They then asked him to make some rules, but he said that he knew nothing about soccer and that it was *their* game, not his. So, with Joe as their facilitator, they began to work out new rules. Once that was accomplished, he asked them how they were going to enforce the rules. After much discussion, they decided that each time they played, four of them would be chosen to act as referees to make sure that the others followed the rules. They then decided the consequences of infringements. Since that meeting, there have been only a few minor injuries. What a great way to teach children the skills of negotiating, setting limits, and respecting the rights of others!

Getting children to express their views and soliciting opinions can generate lots of discussion. I'll ask a child what she considers the most important subject she is learning, then ask another if she agrees with the opinion. If I can get three or four opinions floating around, then I try to get the children to reflect on what the others have said and ask if they agree or disagree. Getting them to listen and respect the thoughts of their fellow students is the kind of experience which will eventually lead to their learning to respect the individual students themselves. Other kinds of questions can lead students to resolving a group problem, as Joe did with his students. Here, students learn a little bit about government, and how no answer is going to satisfy everyone completely, but that each has some part of what she wants in the agreed-to compromises that are eventually reached.

Another type of question involves trying to find an answer for which there is no precedent. An example: "Supposing the character in the book had not been killed, what do you think would have happened?" Another example: "Supposing there were no telephones, how do you think our life would be changed?" This type of approach could help English teachers trying to teach creative writing. As children verbalize ideas and hit upon new ideas as they interact with each other, the experience could help the students understand the whole creative process involved in writing. Thus, the questions you ask should demand on the part of the students some thinking, imagining, and an ability to express an idea which takes a good deal of reflection.

Some parents are concerned that moral values might be taught in student discussions. School is *not* the place, nor could it be, for teaching morality. Children create their values and sense of right and wrong from the experiences they have at home, primarily with their parents and extended family. However, in school, in order to learn, they must be taught to obey rules and to respect the rights of their peers. Thus, there is a need for a program that teaches the children social skills leading to respect for others. The discussions as suggested above are efficient ways to teach children to respect what others say, and, as was mentioned before, they then learn to respect those who speak. Once children learn to respect one another, the chances of children hurting each other decrease, and their chances of learning increase. Topics which deal with moral issues and values are best left for parents to discuss with their children at home.

Speaking of home, this type of social skills training can also be used easily at family gatherings. During the evening meal, when the family is sitting around the dinner table, parents could involve themselves and their children in very lively discussions concerning various topics. Asking children their thoughts, respecting their opinions, not allowing criticism or interruptions when a child is expressing his thoughts—these experiences teach listening skills and respect for others better than all of the lectures parents give when their children are ignoring other family members. And they also create an environment in which children can become self-disciplined and self-confident.

Chapter 7
Setting Rules and Standards

Whether people live together or work together or both, they have to learn to get along. This requires that they cooperate with each other to establish rules and standards upon which they can base their actions. Agreed-to rules allow people to make decisions in ways that do not infringe on others' rights. Standards allow people to go about satisfying their individual goals, sometimes involving direct interaction with other members of the community and sometimes not. In PCT terms, the rules and standards give us direction for how we can control our own perceptions without disturbing others who are trying to control their own perceptions. But, no matter how hard we try, there will be times when we disturb one another. In those cases, rules and standards provide guidelines when resolving the consequences of the disturbances.

Living with others in accordance with standards and rules is something that all children must learn if they are going to be able to function effectively, wherever they live. In family life, in the workplace, on the highway, in stores, and elsewhere, there are always rules and standards, and whether we like it or not, there are always consequences that flow from not following those rules or standards. If I were to walk into a home and mark up the wall with my pen, pick up a dish and throw it onto the floor, or set fire to the sofa, there would certainly be consequences for me. In the community at large, if I drove 55 miles per hour through a school zone, took merchandise from a store without paying for it, or indiscriminately shoved people off a sidewalk, there would certainly be consequences for me.

When a person fails to adhere to rules and standards in a given situation, there usually are consequences for the offender. But often these consequences have little to do with the choices made by the offender. In some cases, the consequences are administered as deterrents to the person's actions and vary in kind depending on who is in charge. Other times, the consequences automatically come into play and those in charge are not allowed discretion. In all cases, consequences are events, good or bad, helpful or not, that occur when people break the rules.

Perceptual control theory shows us that people react to consequences (sometimes called punishments or rewards) based on what they want and how they perceive the situation, not based on what is done to them by others. In short, if they perceive what you've done as a disturbance, then they will act to eliminate any effect you've had. The use of punishments or rewards is not an effective way to control children. For each of us to be able to achieve our own goals in life while interacting with others, we must adhere to the agreed-to rules and standards that allow us to make our own individual choices while respecting the rights of others.

For children to succeed when they go to school, they need to learn to obey rules while, at the same time, respecting the rights of others. This allows them to learn to function not only in the school, but at home, when they get a job, and when they get married and start their own families. If children are taught to deal with life in a way that allows the least amount of hassles and the most satisfaction, then they must learn to respect rules and standards for the reasons they are promulgated, namely as guides to making the best choices while living with others.

The important key to discipline, whether in the home or at school, is that if children persist in breaking the rules, they're given a choice as to whether or not they want to be removed from wherever they are to a more restricted area. Once in the restricted area, be it their bedroom, the school responsible thinking classroom, a chair, or a quiet corner, it still must be their choice as to when they are ready to leave where they are and return. The requirement for returning to where they had been is that they must be willing to work on a plan to deal with others when similar problems arise in the future. *Parents and teachers don't make these choices, the children do.* That is how responsible thinking is taught. They are given the choice, and from this they learn that whatever happens to them is in their hands. (Chapter 8 provides a detailed explanation of this idea.)

Thus, in order for parents to deal with a child, they have to set specific and reasonable rules and standards that must be consistently applied over time and enforced fairly by each parent. On those occasions when children are disruptive and hurtful of others, the parents will then have some already established standards with which to help them deal with these children.

When children are not willing to follow standards or obey rules, they should be asked to name the various choices they have and to explain the consequences that will result from making those choices. The consequences should include the loss of the privileges related to the responsible choice they refuse to make.

Restrictions and loss of privileges must result from their not being willing to work at resolving their problems. Lifting of restrictions and returning privileges should be tied to their having committed to a specific plan to resolve their problems. Trying to control children by rewarding or punishing them not only does not teach responsible thinking, but more importantly, it does not teach them how to creatively work at resolving their problems.

Chapter 8
What Should Happen
When Children Break Rules?

When children refuse to obey rules in any type of social environment, the key to successful discipline is to *offer them choices, so that they can choose where they want to be*. In other words, *they must be given the freedom to choose the level of social contact at which they are willing to act responsibly*. This means that rather than being subject to punitive actions, which usually create more hostility and do little to teach better ways to live in harmony with others, children should, through their *own* choice, experience the loss of the privilege of staying wherever they are until they are willing to accept responsibility for the consequences of their actions.

If children refuse to obey the rules of the classroom or the rules at the dinner table, then they must always be given alternative choices. Perceptual control theory teaches that *we are living control systems* whose behavior is internally driven by the difference between what we *want* to perceive and what we *do* perceive. Thus, teachers and parents must respect their children as control systems that make choices among alternatives. When parents attempt to control these systems, children perceive the attempts as interfering with what they themselves are trying to accomplish. Therefore, children who are disruptive in a classroom or home should be *asked* whether they want to stay in the classroom or wherever they are in the home and obey the rules, or leave.

It is important to remember that children *will deal with those perceived by them to have authority*. If principals constantly undercut the authority of those who work in their buildings, if children perceive bus drivers or substitute teachers or anyone else as having little or no authority over what happens to them, or if a school's core team makes decisions that are ignored by administrators, there will be nothing but conflict. Children *know* who has authority and who doesn't.

The same is true at home. If a mother makes a decision with a child on a certain course of action, but the father undercuts that decision and doesn't insist on the child's accepting responsibility for her acts, then there will be a breakdown of the disciplinary process in that home.

When a group gathers for a common purpose, there is an unspoken agreement to accept the rules and standards common to both the activity and the environment. Whether children are in a restaurant, in a classroom, in a theater, at a football game, or in the home, there are always established rules and standards to follow. The standards are commonly understood, and those who participate with others in the activity give assent to those rules. Respect for the rights of others is part of every culture and is a necessary part of living in harmony with others. Children learn through experience that there are particular rules and standards for each situation. A rule on a school bus might be "stay in your seat." But at play during school recess, vigorous running and jumping would be acceptable and even desirable behaviors. *Whenever children violate the rights of others by refusing to obey the rules and standards of wherever they are, they should be given the choice of being allowed to stay and obey the rules and standards, or leave where they are, reducing their social involvement until they are willing to commit to following the rules and standards and to make a plan to resolve similar problems in the future.*

For every privilege people enjoy, certain responsibilities are demanded. When people cannot act responsibly in particular situations, then they choose to forfeit the associated privileges. I am free to drive on public roads as long as I do not abuse the privilege by running stop signs and traffic lights or by driving at excessive speeds.

When children disrupt and refuse to obey rules, there must be a place for them to go until they are willing to commit to following the rules. This does not mean that children should be made fun of, demeaned, or hurt. I will not work in schools where this happens. Perceptual control theory shows clearly that when you push on a living control system, the reaction of that system is *not based on what you do to that system, but rather on what it wants and how it currently perceives what it is getting.* In other words, people will act to eliminate your effects as a disturbance of perceptions they are trying to control.

The physical destruction of schools correlates with how much school personnel attempt to control children. The more children are offered choices, the less angry they become, and the more willing they are to cooperate with others. That doesn't mean that there won't be pockets of vandalism from some children the schools are unable to reach. However, the overall frequency of vandalism should decrease over time as children sense more control over what happens to them. They become less frustrated. If students feel more relaxed and experience respect from the school personnel, there is bound to be less damage to school property. Perceptual control theory teaches that you *cannot* control another living control system except with physical force. Therefore, the only alternative is to teach children to control their perceptions without acting as disturbances to others. Another name for this is *responsible thinking*.

But how do you structure the choices for students? You have to have a place for children to go where they can sit, calm down, reflect on the choices they have been making, and, if they wish, learn how to make more responsible ones. Perceptual control theory teaches that when people are in conflict, time and patience are needed as they attempt to reorganize their thoughts and decide what they really want. It is important that wherever they go, they be left alone, shown respect, and given the opportunity to sift through their own thoughts. If they seek counsel, it should be given. If they want to be by themselves, leave them alone. Living control systems know what they want and what they can handle. Intruding on a living control system when it doesn't want help is the last thing that should be done. Remember, as has been mentioned before, if you try to push on control systems, they will react according to what is currently important to them, not to what you want. And you can never depend on your own guesses about how other people are going to act when you are perceived as a disturbance to the perceptions they are trying to control.

At home, when children are upset, they should be given the choice of calming down and obeying rules or removing themselves from the social environment of the family. For those children who are in first or second grade or are younger, depending on the strength of the child/parent relationships, the alternative choice should be to sit in a chair, within view of the family or a parent but still far enough removed to allow them to sense the loss of the privilege of being with the family. They should never be demeaned or hurt. In fact, the parents should express confidence in the child's ability to resolve the conflict. Saying such things as "it will work out" or "you're going to make it" expresses to the child the parent's confidence in her ability to succeed and resolve whatever conflict exists. The closer the relationship that children perceive they have with their parents, the more willing they will be to make or accept the choice necessitated by their refusal to obey rules and to get along with the rest of the family.

A critical point comes when the child is allowed to get off the chair and rejoin the family. *When children make this choice, it is because they want to get along in their environment and are willing to work out a plan to make this happen. This plan must resolve how they are going to deal with the same or a similar problem in the future. They have made the choice to act responsibly and join the family. The choice must be their own decision.* When parents make the choice, they aren't teaching their children to make responsible choices, but merely to follow directions.

(Remember, if trying to control children really worked well, you wouldn't be reading this book!)

Another key point is this: *if parents continually make choices for children, who will make responsible choices for those same children when their parents aren't available?* The critical issue is that children must be taught to think for themselves. Otherwise, as they develop and grow, they will not have learned to think responsibly when faced with important decisions. Therefore, it is necessary for children to make the choice and, at the same time, accept the responsibility to work out a plan.

As children grow, so does their ability to handle being totally alone. Thus, once children have matured sufficiently, they should be given the option of going to their room. However, the same principles apply when they want to return: they must commit to resolving the issue, and they must be willing to work out a plan for handling the same problem in the future in a more responsible way.

In school, respecting a child's internal decision-making process is critical. In the primary grades, a quiet corner should be established for children who are disrupting the class. Children choosing to be sent to the quiet corner should never be demeaned or hurt in any way, and the teacher should express confidence in the child's ability to resolve the problem. Just the fact that they take the time and are willing to work with a youngster is evidence to the child that parents and teachers care. This option of choice of removal also can be used in buses, playgrounds, and cafeterias. If a child refuses to settle down in a bus, she could be given the option of respecting the bus rules and remaining where she is, sitting in a front seat opposite the driver until she has demonstrated that she can respect the rules of the bus, or losing the privilege of being on the bus (see Chapter 26). The playground supervisor could have a restricted area close to where she stands; those children who chronically break the rules might be allowed to remain at play, but in the restricted area, with more intensive supervision, until they can demonstrate the necessary responsibility that would allow them the privilege of using the entire field of play, or, for chronic disrupters, allow for a gradual increase in the restricted area as the students demonstrate the necessary responsibility. The cafeteria supervisor might want to have a special table for children near where she is located. Children would have to use that table when they were unwilling to follow the lunchroom rules when eating with their friends.

As children mature, the quiet corner becomes less effective. They need to be given the choice of complete removal from the classroom or, if they are willing to obey rules, remaining. The ideal place for children to go is a classroom where a qualified teacher or counselor works with the disruptive children. I call this the *responsible thinking classroom* (RTC); it is a place where children are taught the necessary skills for getting along elsewhere in the school environment. It is supervised by an adult trained to deal with children, preferably a teacher or another professional. In schools where there are many disruptive children, an additional person, such as a teacher's aide, should serve as monitor; this gives the teacher time to work individually with the children. In schools where an extra teacher is cost-prohibitive, teachers and other qualified staff could take turns in the RTC.

A growing number of children come to school lacking the necessary skills for getting along, for working out ways to cooperate, to set limits, to compromise, and to plan and build and manage their lives. The RTC is a place where children learn the skills needed to get along with their peers and their supervisors (teachers, counselors, and administrators), to make efficient plans, in short to develop the skills of self-discipline. Only children who demonstrate the need for such help should go to this classroom, and they should remain there only as long as they need the help.

It is hard for many to understand the critical need for RTCs in most schools. They do not see the critical need that children have for learning skills for making effective plans, for resolving differences with their peers, for respecting the rights of those in the learning arena, and for practicing self-discipline in social settings in general. Yet the number of children in need of such help is overwhelming the schools of our country, and RTCs can help to solve this problem.

The atmosphere and rules of the RTC are critical. It should not be a place where children are amused or pampered. Nor should it be a room where children are verbally or physically abused or humiliated in any way. Actually, at first it is generally perceived by disruptive children as dull and boring, for there aren't the usual activities found in typical classrooms. As one newcomer to an RTC suggested, "This has got to be the dumbest place I've ever been." In the RTC at Clarendon School, most of the students saw the place as punitive, like a detention room, when they first arrived. Soon, however, they began to perceive it as a place where they were treated with respect and not demeaned in any way—with strict but fair and respectful adults. Then they came to perceive it as a place where they got some intensive and individual help and many chances to succeed. Finally, they perceived it as a place where others care about them.

The rules for the RTC are simple. Students are asked to sit at a desk, and they are not allowed to talk with or disturb other students. I strongly recommend the use of study carrels. Students may stare at a wall, work on a plan to present to the supervisor where they came from, study, or read. They may also put their heads down on their desks and rest or sleep; many students desperately need to rest.

How long should children remain in the RTC? If they choose to leave one teacher and go to the RTC, should they be there during the time they have other teachers with whom they are succeeding? I've found that children should be in the RTC for the time that they have the teacher or supervisor in charge of the place where they chose to leave. With regard to a self-contained classroom, it could be that if the child wants to return and is not a chronic offender, and if the teacher has time to negotiate with the child, then perhaps at a natural break time, such as lunch, the child may be permitted to return to class after having negotiated a plan and resolved the problem with the teacher. The important point here is that the return to class and subsequent negotiation of the plan with the teacher should not be the occasion for another disruption of the classroom.

Another alternative was developed in schools where teachers expressed the concern that students, who had worked out a plan, were missing instruction time while waiting for the teacher to negotiate with them. Once the students had expressed the desire to return to class, to follow the rules, and had worked out a plan with the help and approval of the RTC teacher, they were allowed to return directly to class. However, a special desk was placed inside the classroom, next to the door. The student could quietly open the door, slip into the special "probationary" desk, and could then be exposed to the instruction but would have to wait to participate until there was an appropriate time for the teacher to review and negotiate their plan. If, during the time they were seated at this "probationary" desk, they disrupted, they would give up the privilege of returning to class without benefit of prior negotiations and would choose to return to the RTC.

In the higher grades, where students switch teachers, then the student should be in an RTC only for the time of the class in which he is having difficulty. If students are dealing successfully in one classroom, then they should be allowed to continue in that classroom. They should only be in the RTC for the times they were in class or in other supervised areas where they made the choice to leave rather than get along. Where children are behaving responsibly, depriving them of the opportunity is counterproductive to their development. In short, where they are choosing to make it, leave them alone. Nothing builds success like success. If a child is disrupting in the hallways or walkways, then he should be in the RTC all day, since his areas of disruption cannot be easily separated from where he acts responsibly.

The teacher or supervisor in charge of the RTC is extremely important to the success of the program. At

Clarendon School, I've worked closely with Darleen Martin, a certified teacher, and Becky McNany, a teacher's aide, who are in charge of the RTC. Becky monitors the children and keeps track of their schedules. Darleen works one-on-one with the children, teaching them how to construct plans to present to the supervisors who sent them. Darleen is very good at sensing when and where a child needs help. Parents are often called, and coordinated plans are often made with the children, their teachers, and their parents. Often, make-up work is adjusted to fit a child's plan. For example, children might be afforded some time after school or during recess in the RTC to work on make-up assignments, where ready help comes from Darleen and Becky. To the children at Clarendon, the RTC no longer is a boring place, but a place where someone cares—where they can get help to succeed. One young man who was dealing with an anger problem made a plan to retreat to the RTC whenever he needed to "calm down and get my act together." He also made a "buddy" plan. He had a friend who had a similar anger problem, so they made an agreement that if one started to get angry, the other would attempt to "cool him down" or pull him away from the problem. The last I heard, their mutual plan was working well.

Thus, not only is the RTC a place where children go when they refuse to obey the rules in any school area, but it is also a place where many children develop a growing sense that someone cares: that "I can make it." It becomes a place to catch the disruptive children before things get worse and, with a lot of very creative thinking, to help them turn their lives around. To do this, you need very special people in charge of these rooms—people like Darleen. She literally becomes the conduit for moving the child through the most efficient process for his individual success. With some children, she will work directly with their teachers. With other children, she will sense the need to send them on for personal counseling to the school psychologist or an administrator. With some more recalcitrant children who are unwilling to work things out, she patiently waits them out.

Eventually, all but a very few of those she sees want to resolve their problems, return to where they came from, and *succeed*.

If children disrupt in the RTC, then they should be given the option of acting responsibly where they are, or going home until they are willing to return to school and obey the rules. Some states require that children be suspended for a specific length of time. Regardless of when children return to school, whether according to state law or because they have decided that they want to learn, *they should be returned to the last place that they occupied before they left, namely the RTC*. It just doesn't make sense to mainstream children into other classes if they have yet to make a commitment and a plan to resolve the issues with which they were unwilling to deal before they left (see also Chapter 11). Once in the RTC, the students must work out a plan if they wish to return to the place from which they were originally sent. Again, to allow children into an environment where they haven't learned to get along is setting them up for more failure. The purpose of the RTC is to preserve the integrity of the classroom. To mainstream disruptive students when they haven't demonstrated responsibility in a more restricted environment just doesn't make sense. The other purpose of the RTC is to teach children to become responsible.

When children have been suspended from school or are chronically in the RTC, then a more intense method of involvement between the disruptive youngster and persons who have experience handling difficult situations should be arranged. For this purpose, schools typically use social workers, psychologists, school counselors, or administrators. Regardless of who it is, when children return to school from having been suspended, they should, along with a parent or guardian, meet with the person in charge of discipline. The children should first be asked if they want to work at getting along in school. If they do, then they should work out a plan, which will involve highly intense supervision, and which must be understood by and agreeable to the child, his parents, and the administrator. At first, such children might be sent only to a limited number of classes, or to teachers who are willing to work with them. Of course, the RTC teacher should be involved in all negotiations.

If the returning child is being mainstreamed back to class, then a form should be created which lists, along with the name of the child and the administrator in charge of discipline, those who are going to be supervising the child as she goes through the day. Included on this list should be her teachers and those in charge of the bus she rides, her playground, and her cafeteria. At the beginning of each period, the person in charge is handed the form by the child. At the end of the period, the person in charge signs the form and makes appropriate remarks regarding the child's conduct. At the end of the school day, the child returns to the administrator in charge of discipline, and together they review the day's events. A copy is made of the form and sent home for a parent's signature. This should continue for a minimum of two weeks. The intensity of the twice-daily interaction with the administrator in charge of discipline goes a long way toward helping children succeed.

Finally, children who are absent from class often find themselves far behind the class in subject learning. Once children resolve their conflicts and learn to get along in a classroom, I believe that their prior difficulties should not be held against them. Nor should they be penalized for what they have done, any more than if they had been absent from school due to sickness. Every opportunity should be given to children who have been disruptive to make up their work. Perhaps getting one of the more responsible students to help a student who has fallen behind might benefit both.

Chapter 9
Techniques for Getting
Children to Think

The most important point to remember when dealing with children is that they are, like all of us, living control systems. They have their own wants and goals, they have created their own unique ways of perceiving the world, they make their own choices in trying to change their perceptions to the way they want things to be, and they have their own specific priorities. Thus, dealing with children demands respect for their worlds, and more importantly, understanding how best to help them work through the various difficulties and problems that they have. Since their problems are internal to them, the way you can help them deal with their conflicts is by asking them questions, not by telling them what you think.

The questioning process forces the parent or teacher to stay in the child's world. By asking the right questions, you are teaching children to deal with themselves in such a way as to satisfy their own internal goals. And you are teaching them to do this in the most effective way possible. Lecturing children, telling them what they should be doing, making judgments about what you think is wrong with them—all of these strategies have been tried for years and have never worked. They just make things worse! Any time you push on a control system, you cannot guarantee what it is going to do. And if what you do is perceived by the children as criticism, you're in for a lot of pushing back.

The key in working with children is to ignore excuses, not encourage them. Most counselling time with children is spent arguing over the validity of excuses. A question that should be avoided is "Why did you do it?" When you ask why, you are encouraging children to avoid taking responsibility. Regardless of the why, the key to helping children take responsibility is to stick with the critical elements: what they did, the rules, where they want to be, and what will happen next time they disrupt.

Also, when working with children, try not to be judgmental, which they perceive as an attempt to control them. This works at breaking down the mutual respect you are trying to build. Rather, focus in on the key questions and stay focused. Excuses are an attempt to focus you away from the issue, which is breaking the rules. This method, if followed to the letter, will get you safely past their excuses.

Remember, for children to succeed, they *must believe* you care about them, that you have confidence in their ability to solve problems, and they *must experience respect*. The stronger the relationship before the problems arise (see Chapter 6), the more likely they will accept the process, thus the easier it becomes to resolve the differences. If the questions are asked in a calm, respectful environment, this responsible thinking process can also help build that relationship, because when you ask them what they think, listen nonjudgmentally to their answers, and accept their decisions, this process creates that necessary mutual respect. Remember to ask the questions in a calm, respectful, curious voice. Never yell, lecture, or tell; always ask. Stay focused, and stay with the sequence outlined below until you get familiar enough with the process.

1. "What are you doing?"

Most always, this question should be asked first. Any time children break the rules or don't conform to criteria or guidelines, the focus of concern should always be first the rules or criteria. Once they have agreed that they want to be where they are and are willing to follow the rules to be there, then they have to learn how to stay wherever they want to be. (See Chapter 10.)

There is often a tendency to ask "Why did you do it?" or

"What do you want?" This takes children away from whether they want to follow the rules. "Why did you do it?" leads them to justify their actions. The excuse for breaking the rule is justified by what they want when they are asked "What do you want?" "What are you doing?" begins the process by which you learn if they are ready to accept responsibility.

2. "What are the rules?"

To maintain mutual respect, you have to tie their actions to something outside of you, namely the rules. You're asking them to deal with something that is not a part of you. You'll be perceived as a respectful, interested party, *but not controlling*. You're willing to help them create a workable plan once they've made their decision, but you're not trying to tell them what to do. That's what maintains the mutual respect. Once you yell, tell, argue, or insist on having your own way, they'll perceive you as controlling, and conflict will rear its ugly head.

3. "What happens when you break the rules?"

Here, you are simply getting them to reflect on the consequences of breaking the rules. If there are no consequences, or if they are inconsistently applied, this will have little meaning. They must believe something will happen *every time they break the rules*.

4. "Is this what you want to happen?"

These steps follow logically, but within a short time after their use is begun, *if they are asked consistently*, all that you'll need to use are steps 1 and 6. Most children look to consequences as something that will happen to them. This brings home the fact that, indeed, this *will* happen to them.

5. "Where do you want to be?" or "What do you want to do now?"

This step can be used interchangeably with the prior one. I've introduced a variety of questions to suit various people and situations. The point here is to get closure as to what they really want regarding the conflicting choices they've set up for themselves.

6. "What will happen if you disrupt again?"

This question, along with the first, *should always be asked, even with those children who have caught on to the process*. Reflecting on the future consequences of the same or similar actions is critical for those teaching the art of thinking. It's called thinking ahead. And along with the consequences they might experience, students should also reflect on the unintended consequences to others. Students who disrupt a class keep other children from learning, and might injure or humiliate them. They certainly make it difficult for teachers to keep the class orderly and on task.

If necessary, ask them what they are doing compared to other things they want. This isn't always necessary. The purpose of this comparison is to help the child perceive that although she might be getting some of what she wants when she shoves someone else to the ground, there are other wants that she is being kept from getting, such as being with her friends and playing outside in the playground.

Once they've accepted responsibility for their thinking in a particular area, you then ask them if they are willing to set a goal to work at solving their problems in that area. In PCT terms, you are trying to determine what their goal is, and how hard they are willing to work to make it happen. Once strongly committed to resolving their problems, children are ready to learn how to work out a plan to satisfy what they want using goals and charts (see Chapter 10).

However, in order to learn these techniques properly, you must practice the process *before* dealing with children. The best way to learn the process is by asking some friends to help you rehearse the sequence until you have it well in mind. *The most efficient way is to role-play a totally and completely compliant child:* a child who answers all of your questions truthfully and without any arguments. *This is by far the best and quickest way to learn this process. If you role-play a difficult child or one that offers even the slightest resistance, you will take a much longer time to learn the process. You might not learn it at all. However, once the process is learned with a compliant child, then you'll be able to handle more difficult or resistant children.*

If there are three of you, one should play the child; one should play the teacher, parent, counselor, or administrator; and the third should be the monitor. The job of the monitor is to make sure that the person working with the child follows all of the directions, and also to make sure that the person playing the child is being compliant. I recommend that you make copies of the Responsible Thinking Process card shown in Appendix 1.

The monitor should make sure that the teacher/parent doesn't make any statements, but rather uses *only questions* while dealing with the child. *When you question children, they have to deal with their world, and they are more likely to think responsibly; when you tell children what you think, they stop thinking and rarely follow your directions.*

Going through this process might seem too simplistic. However, if each person in the group takes turns doing each part of the task, after one or two hours of concentrated work, the process will have become quite natural to the participants. They will each think of the sequence without having to refer to the monitor sheet. At that point, playing a child with a little resistance should be tried. *Each step becomes a reference point which you go back to and stay with if the child becomes resistant.* I've watched people become proficient at this process in a single day *after they first experienced role-playing with a person playing a highly compliant child. It is especially important to look for a strong commitment. A weak commitment assures that whatever plan is made, children will be unlikely to fulfill their commitment.*

I've had a mother remark to me after I gave an evening lecture to a parent-teacher meeting at an elementary school that she was headed home to what she thought might be a stormy evening. The next day I met the same woman in the hall of the school and I asked her how things went. She said she arrived home and found seven teenagers in her 15-year-old son's bedroom. He made a flippant remark about how all of his friends were staying the night. She told me that instead of the usual yelling and screaming, she tried what I had suggested. She asked her son what the rule was concerning children staying over night, and he replied, "You're only allowed one person to spend the night." She then asked, "What's the rule about how late your friends can stay?" He replied, "They're supposed to be out of the house by 9:30." She said nothing more and went to the living room to read. About 9:20, she heard some noise in the hallway and asked what was going on. Her son replied, "I'm walking my friends home and Christian is staying the night." She told me, "I couldn't believe it worked. No arguing, no fighting, it was great!"

To help those who want to give this process a try, the following is a typical dialogue between a very compliant child and the RTC teacher.

"Breen, what are you doing in here during recess?"

"The playground supervisor sent me in."

"What were you doing?"

"I pushed Ruth and she fell down."

"What's the rule about pushing children in the playground?"

"You're not allowed to push anyone, and you're supposed to keep your hands to yourself."

"What happens to you when you push children to the ground?"

"You get sent to the responsible thinking classroom, and you're not allowed to play outside during recess."

"Is that what you want to happen, to stay in during recess?"

"No, I don't like being in here."

"What would you rather be doing?"

"I want to be with my friends outside playing."

"Is pushing and shoving children on the playground going to make it possible for you to play outside during recess?"

"No, I'll have to stay inside."

"Is pushing and shoving children against the rules?"

"Yes, it is."

"Do you want to work at solving your problem so you can play outside during recess?"

"Yes, I really do."

"Are you sure you want to work at this?"

"Yes, I really do, I don't like being here in your office."

This is a very simple role-play. In order to learn to deal with more difficult children, you must internalize the process, and this requires dealing at first with very compliant children. Remember, you don't learn to drive on the freeways, you practice on the safer roads first. The same is true with learning this process.

As a teacher or parent establishes the practice of asking the "PCT responsibility questions," most children soon catch on to what she is doing. What develops is this: when the children get disruptive, all that is necessary is to ask "What are you doing?" and the children think through the rest themselves. Often their response is something like "OK, OK, I know," and they straighten themselves up. All you need to do is ask one of the appropriate questions, such as "What are you doing?" or "What's the rule?" Children seem to take over the thinking automatically from just one question and reorganize themselves quickly into following the rules or paying attention to whether or not what they are doing is really going to help them get what they want. However, it is always best, as I mentioned on page 45, to add question 6, "What will happen if you disrupt again?"

The process is simple, yet few understand its unique quality of helping children develop a sense of responsibility within the environments in which they find themselves. And what makes it all so pleasant is that the parent's or teacher's questions are rarely met with anger. Rather, you see the child's own frustration at having to deal with his conflicting goals. When teaching this to parents, teachers, counselors, and administrators, I often say the following: "If you, the parent or teacher, are upset, and your children are relaxed, you're doing it wrong; but if you are relaxed, and your children are showing some frustration or concern, then you're getting it right."

The frustration that children show when they're trying to reconcile what they want with the rules can sometimes make for greater frustration for parents and teachers. My friend Jim Graves told me the story of how his five-year-old son, Aaron, didn't want to finish his dinner. The rule was that if and when an after-dinner treat appeared, there would be none for those who didn't finish their meal. Jim had taken his boy to the park, and instead of stopping by the ice cream parlor as was their usual routine, they walked past. His young son looked up, slightly teary-eyed, pleading with his dad. Jim held firm, although he wanted to give in. As Jim wisely remarked, "It's better that he experience this struggle at a young age than when he is in his teens. The consequence of rescuing children from the struggle is that they haven't learned responsible thinking. What they have learned is that there will always be people to bail them out and excuse them from taking the responsibility for their choices."

Another friend, Mary Kowalski, who is in charge of operations at four residential homes for sexually abused children, explained to me how hard it is to teach a new staff member to hold firm when youngsters who have broken a rule are trying to fight the consequence of being socially restricted until they are willing to make a plan. "It is so hard to watch children struggle and fight to keep from having to deal responsibly with consequences, but every child has got to go through that struggle before they eventually settle down and find harmony within themselves through dealing responsibly with the other children and staff members. It's much harder to teach a staff member to perceive and treat the child as a living control system. They want to manipulate the child, because the staff believes they're not doing their job if they aren't controlling the child. *Trying to teach staff that it is their job to help the child learn the process of thinking and choosing responsibility is so difficult*. Instead, the staff member makes the choice for the child, then tries to convince the child that it's the right choice. But the child only learns to be manipulated, not to think for herself."

This process of teaching responsible thinking is so simple and effective that some children are being taught how to do it, with quite interesting results. George Venetis, principal at Solano Elementary School in the Osborn School District in Phoenix, has been working with Mimi Norton, a sixth grade teacher. She put her children into small groups and then selected a manager to monitor the other students' academic and discipline plans. Throughout the year, each student had the opportunity to take turns being a manager in a group. The idea was to help students help each other succeed. The managers from each group had weekly meetings with their teacher. They'd go out to lunch and talk with Mimi about which student plans were working and which weren't. Mimi asked George to attend the lunches (a local restaurant picked up the tab for the students). However, there was a problem. The student managers felt uncomfortable being "bosses" over other students. George began to teach them responsible thinking techniques which solved the problem: no longer were they *telling* their friends, but they were *asking* instead. This relieved them of the feeling of controlling their friends and put the responsibility back on their friends. They became much more comfortable as managers, and more importantly, their peers began to focus more on their individual plans rather than on seeing the managers as the source of the problems. All of the children are learning to think responsibly and have stopped blaming each other. As they think more responsibly, they act more responsibly.

I remember doing a Saturday training session at Clarendon School with about 60 school personnel and parents in attendance. I had put the participants through a morning training session. After lunch, a middle-aged man announced that "this thing really works." I asked him what happened. He said, "I went home over the lunch hour and my 15-year-old stepson, with whom I don't get along very well, was slouched in front of the TV when he should have been cutting the grass. Usually we get into a big argument. This time I asked him what he was doing, just like you've been teaching us. He said he was watching TV. Restraining my anger, I then asked him what he was supposed to be doing. He then got off his butt, turned off the TV, and went out and started cutting the grass. I call that a miracle!" Once these techniques are learned, you'll find it hard to return to your old style. As one parent remarked to me after two weeks of trying these ideas: "No more yelling and screaming at my kids. I'm so relaxed. How great this is!"

Chapter 10
When Children Want to
Solve Their Problems

Once children are committed to solving their problems, they have to be taught how to make a plan. Regardless of who is working with children, it is the children themselves who have to learn how to resolve the conflicts in their lives.

Plans are not always needed. A first- or second-time offense, involving a minor disturbance, rarely requires a plan. These are often resolved by an adult supervisor asking "What are you doing?" Such "snap counseling" works extremely well with many children, who self-correct when asked about the rules, their goals, or, as in the above example, what they were doing. It also works well with children who know the plan-making process well because of prior experiences.

For children who seem to be developing chronic problems, making a plan is a must. Evaluating the need for a plan is usually easy. If a child cannot on her own create a workable plan, the need is clear. And children with chronic problems will often produce a plan just to get adults "off their backs." At that stage, you should go back to their commitment to resolving their problem and test to see if they are really interested in working things out or are just trying to get rid of you. That is also the time to call in the professional counselors who deal with such children on a daily basis.

The rule is this: when plans consistently fail, then you know there is a weak commitment. And when you challenge the commitment and they are unwilling to make a firm promise to resolve their conflicts, then there is a need for more counselling. Obviously, there are elements in a plan that can make succeeding more likely, but without a firm commitment, there will be no likelihood of achieving success.

As can be seen on the Performance Plan for Improvement (see page 54), there are various areas that must be considered. First, the child has to identify an area for improvement. I suggest that he deal with one problem at a time. What you are really trying to accomplish is to help children build confidence in their ability to resolve the various conflicts in their lives. The smaller the task, the more focused they become, thus the more likely the resolution of the problem, and the better the chance of building confidence. As one friend of mine once suggested, when it comes to helping others make a plan, "think small."

After you have asked a child to establish a specific area of needed improvement, ask her to set a *measurable goal* and create a chart that measures how she is doing. For example, if she wants to improve her reading and decides to read "more than she has been," then that doesn't give her a measurable goal with which to deal. If, instead, she decides to spend one-half-hour reading in her room before dinner and one-half-hour reading in bed before going to sleep on a daily basis, then these are specific times and places and can be easily measured. For her to say "I'm going to read more" is meaningless *unless her announced effort can be measured*. Most children are never taught to make effective plans; therefore, when making any plan with a child, make sure that some type of *measurable* goal is established. Otherwise, there will be no way for the child to measure how well she is doing.

The next critical aspect of plan making is helping children to create detailed outlines for how they are going to accomplish their plans. You'll notice on the Performance Plan for Improvement the need for a "Specific Action Plan." When dealing with children who've been disruptive, it is critical that the teacher find out exactly what happened, including who else was involved and where the children sit in relation to both the teacher and their friends. Thus the children should be asked such questions as "Is sitting next

PERFORMANCE PLAN FOR IMPROVEMENT

PERFORMANCE PLAN BY _____ Date _____

AN AREA OF NEEDED IMPROVEMENT: Explain what you are
presently doing and what you want to be doing in the
future.

_____

_____

_____

MEASURABLE GOAL OR STANDARD: (must tie in to chart
below)

_____

_____

_____

SPECIFIC ACTION PLAN: Detail what you are going to do
to achieve your goal (time, place, days, with whom,
how long, how many). Plan must contain specifics for
measuring progress over time.

_____

_____

_____

                          MEASURABLE GOAL CHART

_____

_____>

_____>

To whom will you report
the progress of your plan? _____

How often? _____ When? _____ Where? _____

Each person's initials _____Date _____

Next meeting - Date _____ Time _____ Place _____

Copyright ©1997 by Ed Ford & Associates

to so-and-so going to help you remain quiet?" and "Is sitting in the back row the best place to help you achieve your plan?" The more specific you get, the fewer problems will be faced when the child attempts to put the plan into action. If children are going to establish a plan for doing more homework, then questions have to be asked about the details. Where are they going to study? With whom and at what time? Will the TV or radio be on? What if someone stops by to play? Will they be taking phone calls? The more details considered, the less likely the failure of the plan.

As I discussed earlier, there is a need for both a specific goal and a record of how we are doing relative to that goal—thus the necessity of a chart that reflects exactly what we are doing so we can accurately judge whether we are achieving our goal. The top diagram on page 56 is a chart consistent with perceptual control theory. The goal represents what we want. As we mark down how much time we spend on our activity, what we begin to see is the historical representation of how we've been doing. When you look at this chart, you are literally comparing your goal with how close you are to achieving your goal—exactly the way that our brains function. The difference between your goal and how close you've come to achieving your goal is what drives you to work at improving. In other words, you want something, and you presently perceive the status of what you want. Your actions are merely to change that status to conform to what you want. That's what *thinking* is all about, and that's perceptual control.

For a child who has been talking in class or getting out of her chair without permission, reaching the goal should represent success at a plan. Thus, the top parallel line would be the "success" line. Another line halfway down the chart would be marked "needs to improve." The time increment should be what the child can presently tolerate. A talkative child might be set at 10- or 15-minute intervals. If the child succeeds at this increment, then the amount of time should be increased slowly, according to the child's ability to demonstrate responsibility. *It is better to give short increments of time so that the child has a better chance of experiencing success.*

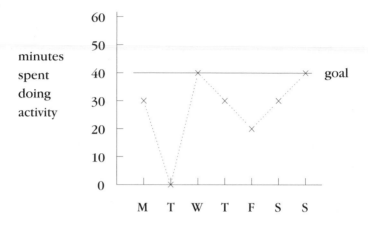

days of the week

Another type of goal line would be a diagonal line. Thus, a child making a plan to read 100 pages in a week could see her progress each day and compare that to where she should be if she actually read the number of pages each day that would allow her to reach her goal. See below.

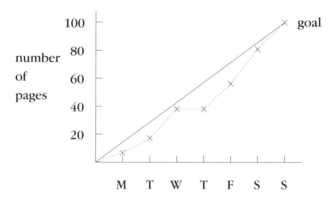

days of the week

You'll notice on each of the plan sheets shown in this chapter that there is a provision for "touching base" with a teacher or parent. The more involved a parent or teacher is in the making and executing of a plan, the less likely children are to fail. And that is what this whole process is all about, helping children to achieve success. Having the child touch base with you on a regular basis as he works through the process of completing the plan tells him that you care, that you are interested enough to take the time to find out how he is doing. That is the best way to show children you care; not by telling them you do or giving them little pep talks, but by being there and showing an interest as they report to you how well they are doing. You represent an important part of their success, that part where someone is interested and caring. And that is what building a close relationship with a disruptive child is all about.

Joe Sierzenga, former principal of Morrice Elementary School in Michigan, told me of helping an entire class improve their grades by using plan making and a chart. Joe and Ronneal Jenison, a sixth grade teacher, successfully increased the grade point average of every child in her class, some going from failing to honor roll. Student attitudes improved due to the tremendous improvement in grades, and there was better utilization of class time because of increased student work output.

First, Joe and Ronneal met with each interested parent to see if improving their child's grade point average was something that they wanted to get involved with. Once the parents were committed, Joe met individually with each student. Some students whose parents showed no willingness to participate requested on their own to be part of the program.

Next, Joe and Ronneal met individually with the students and interested parents to establish a measurable goal of how many minutes per night each student was going to study. They then created a specific plan for each child. This plan included such details as when they would study (this was the most important criterion), which days (including weekends), where they would work, with whom, and whether TV, the phone, radio, or visitors would be allowed. Joe acted as a facilitator between parents and their children, training them to work cooperatively to create the plans. Joe helped them create goal charts (see performance plan on page 54), and he gave copies to both the parents and children. Finally, each child wrote down the consequences as to when they would make up the time if they failed to achieve their plan on any evening (this might involve doing their work during recess at school or immediately upon arrival at home).

Every day, the students came into class, handed in their homework, and logged in whether they had achieved their study-time goals on their charts in their classroom. This was also done on their charts at home. Subsequent meetings were held based on their charts in the classroom and the daily student assignment sheets, which the parent would sign certifying the time spent by the children. Any problems with information on the charts would bring a prompt meeting with the students, their parents and teachers, and Joe. If there was no homework, they would still have to spend the committed time doing a school-related activity, usually reading. This got around students trying to avoid doing their homework, since this study time was committed whether they had homework or not.

On the following pages are two kinds of plan sheets, one suited for primary grade children and the other for older children. After looking at these, you might want to make your own.

MY PLAN

Name _____

Date _____

What did I do?

What rule did I break?

What happens when I
break the rules?

Do I want that to happen?
Yes _____   No _____

What would I rather
have happen?

Is what I am doing
getting me what I want?
Yes _____   No _____

Am I willing to work at
making things better?
Yes _____   No _____

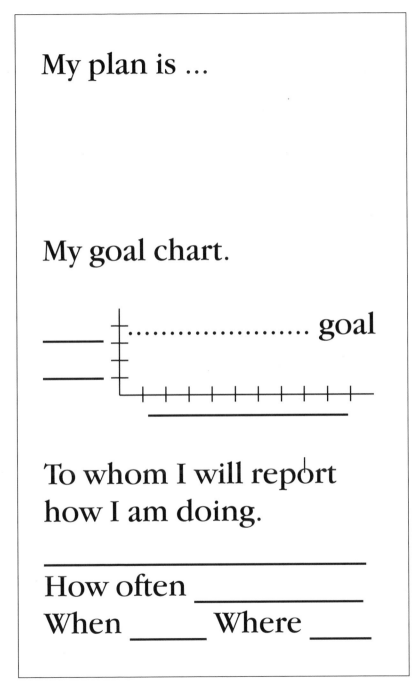

My plan is ...

My goal chart.

_____ ┼.................... goal

_____ └┼─┼─┼─┼─┼─┼─┼─┼─┼─
      _____

To whom I will report
how I am doing.

_____

How often _____
When _____ Where _____

STUDENT PLAN - RESPONSIBLE THINKING CLASSROOM

What would the person who was in charge of where you came from say you were doing?

_____

What was the first question that person asked you?

_____

What was your answer to the question?

_____

What would you say you were doing?

_____

What is the rule that you broke?

_____

At the time you broke the rule, did that keep other students from doing things they were trying to do?   Yes   No

What were some of the things you kept them from doing?

_____

Did you keep the person in charge from doing something?   Yes   No

What was the person trying to do?

_____

When a person is called responsible, what does that mean?

_____

_____

What are the good things about being a responsible person?

_____

What things don't you like about being a responsible person?

_____

Would you say that you are responsible (circle one)

    most of the time   half of the time   very little of the time

Would you like to work on a plan that would help you become more responsible?   Yes   No

How many times have you written a plan to work on becoming more responsible?   _____

How will the person where you disrupted know you are serious about working on a plan to be responsible?

_____

_____

Please write your new plan. _____

_____

_____

_____

Will you keep other students or your teacher from doing what they
are trying to do if you follow your plan?   Yes   No

Please explain. _____

_____

What is different about this plan from your other plans?

_____

_____

What is your plan to make up the school work you've missed?

_____

_____

If you want help, where or from whom can you get it?

_____

How can the person in charge of where you were disrupting help you
with your plan?

_____

Are you really serious about working on your plan?   Yes   No

Will a monitor sheet or chart help with your plan?   Yes   No

If so, create a chart or monitor sheet that will help you
keep a daily record of how you are doing.

_____   _____
student's signature   RTC teacher

_____   _____
person in charge of where   parent signature
   disruption took place   (when necessary)

Once you have negotiated this plan with the person who was in charge
of the place where you were disrupting, and that person has signed
the plan, return this plan to the RTC teacher and you will be
released from the RTC.

Chapter 11
Dealing with Children
Who Continually Break Rules

A major frustration of both parents and teachers is in dealing with children who are chronic offenders, those who repeatedly disrupt. These children often make convincing verbal commitments and show great remorse, with a sincerity that would melt the hearts of all but the toughest prison guards. Still, when returned to the environment from which they chose to leave due to their disruptive behavior, they soon revert to their irresponsible acting out. To deal with these children, I suggest the following:

1. First, look at their relationships, especially with their parents. This is by far the most important area. The quality time (see Chapter 6) that parents spend with their children is the most critical factor when it comes to children building confidence in themselves and believing that someone has confidence in their ability to succeed.

Often schools can do little because they are overwhelmed by so many children, especially if parents do little to cooperate with the school personnel. Student class discussions are important, but there is no substitute for quality time. If schools could develop a corps of volunteers who would be willing to spend time with students having problems, this would be a step toward helping children develop the all-important self-confidence that's so closely tied to warm, loving relationships.

2. There is a need for consistency in how children are treated. This means similar training in counselling techniques for both parents and school personnel. Entire staffs

can and should be trained so that everyone treats children in the same way by asking questions that help them to think responsibly. The techniques suggested earlier in this book can be learned by most people in a day or two of intensive training.

3. There should be in place an alternative choice, a place for disruptive children to go: in the home, a chair or, for older children, their bedrooms; in schools, a supervised area, such as the RTC, where they remain until they are willing to learn how to work things out with the person in charge of where they were being disruptive.

4. An adequate plan should be in place, one that has a measurable goal, using a chart. The plan should have a specific detailed outline for how it is going to be carried out, with various possible problems anticipated. For example, will the plan allow for phone calls, or personal visits by a friend?

Even with all of the above in place, there still remain some major problems with children who chronically misbehave. At home, children are sent to their rooms or restricted to the home; at school, they are thrown out of class, suspended, given detention, or even expelled. The frustration can be easily seen in the faces of administrators, counselors, and teachers in many of our schools today.

A major problem is that children might be permitted, after their period of "time-out," to be *mainstreamed back to wherever they came from without having first demonstrated responsible thinking at intermediate steps*.

Several years ago, I worked as a consultant at one of Arizona's major juvenile lock-up facilities. The young offenders were housed in small units that held about 15 to 20 teenagers. Occasionally, a fight would break out and the guards were called to take the young man to lock-down, where he was placed in a cell by himself until he calmed down. Once it was decided that the young man was no longer a danger to himself or others, he would be returned to his unit. That procedure didn't make sense to me. I suggested to the superintendent that he establish a transition unit with intense counselling and supervision, in which the juveniles' freedom was far more restricted than the regular units, but less so than the lock-down unit. I thought they should be placed there until they could demonstrate their ability to deal responsibly with the rules and their fellow inmates, prior to being allowed to return to their regular unit. What happened when a trial transition unit was established? The number of outbursts in the various units was dramatically reduced.

I had a similar experience when I was a consultant in a hospital for the criminally insane. I was working on what was called the strong ward, which housed the most dangerous men. They were housed in individual cells and were allowed in the day hall for only two hours in the morning and two hours in the afternoon. If a man became violent, the day attendants, eight on both the day and afternoon shifts, would take a mattress, pin the offender to the wall or floor, and his arms and legs would be strapped to the four corners of his bed until he had calmed down. After several days of demonstrating more rational behavior in his cell, he would be allowed full time in the day hall. Invariably, within a few days to a few weeks, he would disrupt again. He had never experienced the necessary success that builds self-confidence. He needed to learn how to build confidence through responsible thinking. I implemented a program where the attendants would individually spend time visiting each inmate for 15 minutes twice daily, building individual relationships with the inmates. I also created a program where violent prisoners would have to demonstrate responsibility in their cells, by mopping the floor, cleaning the wash basin and toilet bowl, and talking in a sane and respectful manner. After several days of this, we would allow them in the day hall for 15 minutes in the morning and 15 minutes in the afternoon. Sometimes, with the more fragile inmates, I would have them sit next to the attendant in charge. They were more at ease when they were next to the attendant. Every two or three days, we would increase their time in the day hall by short increments, from 15 minutes to a half hour, then to an hour. Finally, after several weeks, they would be allowed the full two hours. What happened? The number of incidents was reduced.

This gradual approach to full responsibility can be used anywhere there is disruptive behavior. At home, after children have been sent to a chair, they might be required to play by themselves, away from others. Or they might be required to play near a supervising adult. I have found that, if children are placed near an adult whom they like and to whom they feel close, they tend to handle themselves more responsibly. The adult is perceived as a source of strength and security by children having difficulty following rules. Thus, being near such an adult makes it easier for children to reconcile their problems.

Another option for parents is that the offending children might play with a more responsible child or play in a restricted area of the house or yard. And the same would apply to children who are old enough to be sent to their rooms. They can spend time by themselves learning to use their minds by reading or becoming involved in a hobby or project around the house. Sometimes going for a walk or bike ride with a child is helpful, or engaging them in some activity that you are involved in, such as cooking, washing the car, or repairing something around the house.

At school, traditional methods of discipline follow a cause-effect model. What can we do to children to get them to behave? With this ineffective method, once the children have been punished by being suspended and returned or serving detention, they are often forgotten until the next event. There is a silent hope among administrators that somehow the children will have "learned their lesson" and they will "straighten out." But not only have the children not committed themselves or made a plan, they haven't demonstrated any kind of responsibility. Yet they are allowed to go back to class or to another group setting.

Chronic offenders in the primary grades can spend time in the corner of the room. When they are willing to work things out, they might be allowed short increments of time with the class, with the remaining time in the corner. I've found that when responsibility is demanded of chronic offenders, the shorter the time increments, the greater the chance of their being successful. Another alternative for continually disruptive children is to seat them in one of the front seats, or a special place literally right next to the teacher's desk. Or they could be placed next to more responsible children, who wouldn't be as tempted to get involved in the irresponsibility of the offending child. How long the child should be seated in a special place depends on the strength of the child, and this has to be a judgment call on the part of the teacher.

The RTC is a place where the children have to demonstrate their willingness to follow rules. They should never be returned to class until they have made a plan with the supervising teacher. And when a child returns to her class or wherever she came from, *she must negotiate with the adult in charge*. To be able to return and not have to plan how to handle future similar problems defeats the whole purpose of teaching children responsibility.

In the case of children who are chronic offenders, they might be allowed back with their class or group only for short periods of time. The balance of the time would be spent in the responsible thinking classroom. Some might argue that the children are losing valuable class time. My answer is that if they were in class *before they were ready*, others in the class would not be learning, because of the ongoing disruption.

When chronic offenders return from the RTC, one plan might be to not allow them to return to where they had been seated, surrounded by their friends. They should be seated in the front of the room. If possible, they should be seated with the more responsible students. These are things that would allow these misbehaving students to demonstrate their willingness to follow rules.

The bottom line is this: for children to be full-time in class, they must have demonstrated their ability to obey rules in a gradually less restricted environment. This will (a) promote success, (b) protect others who are learning, and (c) insure uninterrupted learning for those who are respecting the rights of others.

The same caution is true for other places than in classrooms. Whether it be in the bus, the cafeteria, the playground, the gym, or wherever, the chronically disruptive children should not be sent directly back from a responsible thinking classroom without some kind of restriction as to where they may sit or move about. If a child has been acting out in a bus, he shouldn't be allowed to sit in the back of the bus until he has demonstrated that he can take responsibility in a more highly supervised area, which, in the case of the bus, could be in the front seat, across from the driver. In this way, he can show by the way he handles himself that he is ready for less restrictive seating (see Chapter 26). The same pattern would apply in the cafeteria. A table located close to a cafeteria supervisor should be provided. Disruptive children would be allowed to sit in the cafeteria at that table only after they have made the commitment to take responsibility for behaving well in the cafeteria. Only after they have demonstrated responsibility at this restricted table for an appropriate period of time should they be allowed to eat with their friends. Other alternatives could include eating in a restricted area next to the cafeteria, or sitting with or near a teacher. And, again, they should be restricted to these places for as long as they continue with even the slightest amount of disruption. Also, when chronically disruptive children return after lunch to recess, their area of play should be close to where the supervisor stands. Perhaps the first time, the restricted area could be right next to the supervisor; a week later, it could be extended further away. Also, predetermined responsible friends or a reduced number of their own friends could be allowed with the child in the restricted area.

It's important to remember that the number of days in restricted areas should depend on how well the children demonstrate their ability to handle freedom. The more they show that they can handle responsibility, the more assured the parent or teacher is that there will be less chance of future disruptions.

Whenever there is a repeat offense, the rule is that the person remains in the restricted place longer. The disruption demonstrates that apparently the child didn't have enough time to build the necessary self-confidence to demonstrate responsibility. Thus, the more chronic the offenders, the slower they should be returned, and the more they should demonstrate their willingness and ability to follow the rules. This isn't to make the child suffer, but rather to assure the child's success. The only thing that builds self-confidence in children is to succeed in the area in which they are trying to improve.

The Intervention Team

Over the past three and a half years this program has been used, the major complaint of teachers and administrators is the chronic, repeat offenders, often referred to as "frequent fliers." This is common in all schools. Although the number of frequent fliers seems high, in schools using RTP for half a year, they comprise a small number. In a typical elementary school of 625 students, about 400 never go to the RTC, 170 go only once, and 40 show up anywhere from two to six times. Between 10 and 15 students, about two to four percent of the school population, are serious problem children. In my experience, all of them come from highly dysfunctional homes.

When children begin to make repeat visits to the RTC, an intervention team should be called. The purpose of this team is to help the children succeed. Another purpose of the team is to evaluate initially who would be the most effective person or persons to deal with the child. Members of the team should include the parents, the RTP administrator, the RTC teacher, the student's teacher, and appropriate support resource persons within the school (possibly including the coach or others who know the student well) and, if needed, within the school district or community. In residential settings, the team should include dorm or unit staff and/or mentors. It might be helpful to ask the children if they have any suggestions for the team. Also, they might be asked who they would like to work with. The more children perceive a person as caring, the more likely they will be willing to work with that person. And who would know better than the child himself?

Students who begin to show up in the RTC more than two or three times, especially within a week, need the support and help of the intervention team. The child should never be seen as a problem, but rather as a challenge, someone who needs team support. He might need the help of the school psychologist, or family visits by the appropriate person from the school, such as the social worker, or he might find the solution in a community program specifically designed for him. This intervention team should meet, record what it is doing, and, when needed, seek the help of outside resources.

Too often, children who continually disrupt tend to get a larger dose of punishment. Instead of a day's suspension, five or 10 days are given out, all with the idea that somehow being more punitive is going to teach children how to resolve all of their problems and work through the difficulties with which many are overwhelmed. I've known many cases where children who have lived in homes where murder and rape have been witnessed, where they themselves have been sold to adults for sexual pleasure, where beatings are so severe that they come to school with raw and open sores. And yet these children are expected to know how to act responsibly, think on their own, while being screamed at, punished, and humiliated, all in the name of trying to get them to behave. Only an intervention team with sympathetic members can work with the students and, if they are willing, their parents, to help the children succeed in the one area which can offer them some hope for the future, namely an education. The way school staff handle the more difficult students is a measure of how well they understand and use the responsible thinking process.

The intervention team is especially well suited for the various people who service children within the school building: the school psychologist, the social worker, the guidance counselor, the nurse, and the administrative staff. It gives everyone a role in the intervention process, tied directly to the specific skills that each person brings to the team and what is appropriate for the child. And it allows everyone to center their attention on the most needy children.

Chapter 12
Knowing Your Limitations

One of my favorite lines from Clint Eastwood's many "Dirty Harry" movies was in "Magnum Force." His supervisor remarked that he had never had to pull his gun from its holster. Harry replied, "Well, you're a good man, lieutenant, and a good man always knows his limitations." This line is certainly appropriate to parents and school personnel in their struggle to work with children. PCT teaches us about our limits with regard to dealing with other living control systems.

Recently, I was teaching a course on discipline to bus drivers. One of the bus drivers told how one time, while driving, he was hit on the back of his head with paper clips. Immediately, the children started laughing, jumping out of their seats, and sticking their heads out the windows. When he could, he safely pulled over to the side of the road, turned the motor off, removed the key, got off the bus, and took three or four deep breaths. He said he wanted to get his emotional state calmed sufficiently so that he could deal reasonably and rationally with the children. Then he got back on the bus and announced to the children that they had two choices: remain where they were until the authorities arrived (his bus had a two-way radio) or be driven home. They immediately calmed down and chose to go home.

I have discovered that, when working with children, if the supervising adult is upset and the children are relaxed, then the adult is doing something wrong. The children should be doing the thinking and showing concern, and the adult should be relaxed. As described earlier, asking questions to generate thinking is the most efficient way of handling children and is very consistent with PCT, because you are not trying to control their actions, thus they are less likely to perceive you as a disturbance.

Children can resolve their own problems, but only when their inner world is calm, so that they are willing to deal with the questions being asked. There are times when children don't calm down, for whatever the reason. Such behavior makes a critical difference: you cannot work with children who refuse you access to their worlds. There are definite limits to what you can or cannot do. If a child is determined to disrupt, there is nothing *anyone* can do, short of applying overwhelming physical force.

School districts have a ratio of anywhere from six to 15 children to one staff member. The administrators are not equipped to handle highly delinquent children. They do not have the physical resources and staff to handle the very intense type of individual work that is often needed with seriously disruptive juveniles. When a child refuses to cooperate in a school or in any way threatens the safety of children or adults, then the police should be called—they have been trained to handle such situations. Teachers and administrators who try to resort to physically restraining children open themselves to liability and are acting outside of the scope of their jobs. More importantly, *school children should never be exposed to these types of highly disruptive individuals.* I know of one school where a teacher's aide was assigned the task of following a youngster around all day, wherever he went. This child was known for attacking other students in a highly aggressive way. For a school district to expose their children to this type of dangerous acting-out individual is very wrong.

Such children need to be placed in residential treatment centers, where there are usually one to two staff members to every one juvenile. Even residential treatment centers cannot cope with certain dangerous children, who require lock-up facilities. There, these extremely disruptive juveniles have a specially trained staff to work with them. Again, school personnel should not attempt to deal with children they are not competent to handle, because they lack the resources or training. These children should be sent to where there is adequate help available. All those in the business of helping children have to know their limits and admit to themselves and their colleagues what they can and cannot do.

Too often a community expects more from a school than it has the staff and resources to accomplish. It is not that the teachers, counselors, and administrators are incompetent, but that they are expected to deal with children in an inappropriate setting, with a staff lacking the needed training.

Parents, too, are often overwhelmed by disruptive children. Recently, in my home town of Phoenix, a former mayor suggested that the financial liability of parents for damage done by their children be increased substantially as a way of controlling the vandalism of children. Going after parents by making them financially liable just gives a handle to acting-out teenagers for "getting even" with their parents by destroying property, thus creating liabilities for the parents which their children can hold over the heads of their parents as a way of getting the parents to acquiesce to their children's demands. The courts have the police and lock-up facilities to protect them, schools have the right to suspend children, but, at least in Arizona, there are no laws that give parents protection from acting-out children who refuse to obey the rules and laws of the community. Thus, parents have no recourse or protection from highly destructive children. And I am not talking here about the kind of parents who abuse or neglect their children. I'm referring to those parents who are trying to do their best, and yet are at a complete loss as to which way to turn. Holding parents financially liable as the mayor suggested gives zero relief to frustrated parents and, indeed, teaches nothing. These parents often find their homes in utter chaos, and generally with tragic results.

What is needed is cooperation, not conflict. Parents have to begin to perceive their children's school as a place where everyone works together. Teachers have to view parents as resources for helping the children to succeed. And the school administrators, counselors, school psychologists, social workers, district office administrators, and school board members have to be catalysts for making it all happen. They have to create the kind of cooperative atmosphere where everyone works toward the same common goal—the success of the children.

Increasing the financial liability on parents with acting-out children, as the former Phoenix mayor suggested, teaches nothing and contributes to the chaos we now have in many of our schools, homes, and communities. With PCT as the guiding theoretical basis for what we do, everyone has to join together and align their goals and plans. Then, with everyone working together, we can help schools and our children create the kind of learning environment in which everyone wins.

Chapter 13
Keeping the Program Alive

I have been to a school where, after my two-day awareness and skills training program, the usual excitement began to build as the teachers and parents found the techniques they'd been taught "really work," but there was no follow-through, no organized way to make sure that the program continued. And there was no organized way to handle all of the various problems inherent in such a project. In another district, I worked on a regular basis as a consultant for a month or so in an elementary school, and the program was going well, with fighting, special education referrals, vandalism, and student disruptions on the decline. Then, the following year, the district office moved the principal, the assistant principal went back into the classroom, and the whole program collapsed.

To insure survival of a successful discipline program at a school, a strong core team representing the entire school and the parents of the children attending the school is absolutely critical. This group should include key members of the administrative staff, especially the RTP administrator and the RTC teacher, as well as the school counselor, psychologist, representative teachers, and several parents, preferably those representing the parent-teacher organization.

All members of the team must *assume ownership* of the program from its creation. They must assume ownership by taking active roles in formulating standards and by monitoring the program on a regular basis. The RTP administrator and the RTC teacher must continue to give the team information on the number of children needing help, the number of repeats, any special difficulties, and where extra help is needed (such as when there are unsupportive teachers). In short, everyone has to take pride of ownership in the program—and show off that pride to others. This is especially important for parents, as they talk with friends in the school's community and with school board members, so that everyone can become better acquainted with the program.

The core team must regularly clarify expectations and should never assume that everything is running smoothly, especially given ongoing staff and parent turnover. At the beginning of each school year, specific objectives should be established. Throughout the year, each team member should visit the RTC, demonstrating support for those on the "front lines." There must be *constant updating and clarification* of what is being done, and continuing re-dedication in terms of their support for the RTP administrator, how the team functions in relation to the program itself, and what each member's role is for giving individual support.

When the team meets, there needs to be an agenda. For each item on the agenda, one or two individual team members have to be willing to take responsibility for seeing that the particular item is researched and reviewed by appropriate people at the school and, if necessary, by the district office. At each meeting, the team should review each item on the agenda, getting an update on its present status. No item should be ignored or removed without appropriate team action. The team's job is to process ideas and make decisions. Endless discussions should not eat up the core team's time. Rather, let meetings of those interested in specific items take place elsewhere, and let the person responsible for the item create a consensus upon which the core team can make a decision. But the responsibility for the final decision as to how each item is to be resolved should always be in the hands of the core team.

At the beginning of any major change in how a school functions, such as the installation of a new discipline program including an RTC, the team should meet once a week for about an hour (it is better to increase the frequency of the meetings than their length) to evaluate the program and to look for ways to improve it. Eventually, teachers will begin to understand the program—especially its non-punitive approach to dealing with children—and perceive the benefits. It will take at least two or more months to work through the various difficulties that invariably arise before the system is running smoothly. Everyone has to be involved, everyone has to care, and everyone has to take ownership if the program is going to succeed; that means parents, teachers, the entire school staff, and the district office support personnel as well.

One way to make sure RTP continues to succeed is by having parents as active members of the core team. Schools are highly sensitive political animals; if any worthwhile program is to survive, the parents must participate in the decision-making process of the program. Also, this allows constant input by the parent representatives to the parent-teacher organization as to how the program is going, and the opportunity to respond to those individual concerns parents might have. With parental input into the program from the very beginning, the aura of secrecy and subsequent criticisms and suspicions will never arise.

Discipline programs at home need to grow and prosper along with school programs. Like the school core team, the key for parents is first and foremost the strength of their relationship, where there are two parents, and the strength of the relationship of the individual children with each of their parents, regardless of whether the parents are living together or not. Parents are the core team at home. Often this might include older responsible siblings or another member of the family, such as a grandparent. Without strong, ongoing, healthy adult relationships in which everyone works cooperatively together, children lack the critical support needed to build confidence in their ability to create the necessary self-confidence for success.

Parents should constantly evaluate, both alone and occasionally with their children, how things are going. The key in both home and school is the constant reporting to those who are involved about how things are going. This updating allows a quick response from those in charge to take care of any concerns that might arise. The strength of families will determine, in large part, the strength of any school discipline program. The stronger the family relationships, the better equipped are children to handle the various conflicts that arise at school.

The core team is the catalyst for getting RTP started. Once implemented, the team should support the RTP administrator and the RTC teacher in every way possible. But the team's unique role is to promote ownership of the program by the entire community, which means the school staff and the parents. A danger of a core team is that it can restrict power to itself, becoming a quasi-administrative power group. The core team should monitor, help renew, and keep vital the discipline program, *but it must always recognize that it is responsible to the community of parents and the staff of the school.* The team's accountability to the rest of the staff and the school parents is critical. *When the community owns and values any program within the school, it won't let it go. The role of the core team is to make sure that happens.*

Chapter 14
Dealing with Objections

Some individuals who have not tried the techniques suggested in this book can be expected to raise certain common objections which deserve answers. Rather than burden the rest of the book with these arguments, I have gathered them together in this chapter. Here I hope that you will find the help you need if, when you try out some of my suggestions, someone who has not read this book criticizes what you are attempting to do.

1. Some might claim that I begin with the conventional view of discipline as the exertion of power by some people over others, in the guise of imposing rules.

The rules necessary to enable learning in the classroom and harmony at home are *not* arbitrary impositions, and children—even when very young—generally understand the importance *to themselves* as well as to others of having established, accepted rules. They understand the *purposes* behind the rules and the *need* to have them. (See Chapter 7 for a discussion of rules in terms of PCT.)

Not long ago, I asked some of my grandchildren why there are rules in school. Their answers were as follows: Five-year-old Nelson: "So you don't hit anybody"; seven-year-old Ruth: "So you don't get in trouble"; 10-year-old Hester: "So the world won't be a crazy place in which to live"; 11-year-old Thomas: "So no one will get hurt." An hour or so later, other grandchildren (we have 18) were gathered together, and one of them suggested that they play with a ball. Immediately, one of them said, "Before we play, we have to make some rules."

On another occasion, I held class discussions with students at second, third, fifth, and sixth grade levels. Those in the latter three grades seemed to understand that following rules that they didn't like would allow them to be where they *wanted to be*, and that it was worthwhile to follow the rules for that purpose. When pressed for examples, they offered such places as their home, at school, on the bus, on the playground, in the school cafeteria, and visiting at a friend's house. These children recognized the need to sometimes follow rules with which they might not agree. They also said that other children know when they are wrong, and that they are responsible for what they are doing. (In my student discussions, I never make overt judgments, nor do I try to influence the students' comments in any way.)

I have often asked in my discussions with students, "Why do some children always seem to get into trouble?" The answer, universally, has been, "So they can get attention." Most people follow rules out of respect for those who live in the environment where they find themselves. As I stated above, most children not only agree that rules are necessary, they know and accept them. *I've found that while secure children live happily with rules, insecure children have difficulty following rules, because they are attempting to satisfy their internal goals of wanting to be cared about without respecting the rights of others.* As the children themselves will tell you, they are trying to get attention. When I pressed one group of children as to why a child would break school rules in order to get attention, one child wisely remarked, "I guess he couldn't figure out how to get attention by getting along with others."

2. Some might express disappointment that I don't emphasize examining the particulars of the rules themselves, considering the kinds of rules that children generally will accept, and the kinds that they generally will reject.

Again, I am concerned with *established* rules, already *accepted* by most of the children in a given situation as there for good reasons. Children learn rules in the give and take of life. For example, a child interrupts her parent and the parent says, "Don't interrupt, I'm trying to talk." After several such interruptions, I just ask, "What's the rule about interrupting people when they're trying to talk?" If my relationship with the child is sufficiently warm, the child generally tells me the rule, walks away, and the problem is resolved. That way, children think through what they were doing and then go about doing something else.

A rule like "no talking in class" is made so that the teacher can teach and those children interested in learning can learn. Children who are disruptive lack the common courtesy needed for people to function together. When a child's goals and consequent actions violate the common goals of the group (in school, all of the other children working with the teacher), those others' rights are being violated. A child's individual rights *do not* allow the disruption of the community. In learning to follow rules established for the social good, a child needn't give up all of her own goals but must learn to respect the others. The real purpose of rules is to allow people to live in harmony with each other while satisfying their own goals.

3. Some might argue as follows. You can talk all you want about offering choices, but if the only real choice given a child is between obeying a rule and having her freedom (or anything else) taken away, then the child is being punished, no matter what you call it. A genuine choice has at least one attractive alternative.

The above definition of punishment is quite different from mine. I consider punishment to be hurting others—forcing them without giving them a choice, verbally abusing them, or doing something to them "to get them to change." The method of discipline discussed in this book offers children the choices that, in the circumstances in which they find themselves, are the *only* ones open to them—the *only* choices possible, given their current situation.

Also, a genuine choice need *not* necessarily have at least one attractive alternative. (Try not paying your taxes!) People are faced with choices where there are no attractive alternatives all of the time. And there are plenty of occasions where there are only unhappy choices, but with a higher good being achieved. The child making the choice of following a rule he doesn't like, such as talking out of turn or shoving children who get in his way, achieves a higher goal of being allowed to stay with his friends and to learn in the safety of the classroom or play in the safety of the playground.

If children perceived what I recommend doing as punitive, they wouldn't get *less* upset, but instead *more* upset. My discipline program has proven to result in less fighting, less damage to the schools, and less disruption. In short, the results are most encouraging for everyone, including the children. Schools that have punitive programs—and most do—really have serious problems, including lots of physical damage to school property.

Children *do not* perceive what I suggest doing as mean or unfair. I can't remember a single child getting more upset than before. And the best evidence comes from parents trying these ideas in their homes. I am talking about scores of parents, all enthusiastic about the results.

4. Some might ask for more emphasis on helping children to achieve self-discipline, by engaging them in the rule-making process and by debating the worth of existing rules.

I believe that self-discipline *begins* with learning the discipline of getting along with others. Self-discipline is exactly what I am pointing toward. In PCT terms, self-discipline does not mean controlling our behavior. Rather, it means controlling our perceptions in such a way that we minimize the disturbances we create for others.

Self-discipline demands not only respect for others, but also the ability to set one's own standards and live by them. If those standards conflict with the standards of the community in which one lives, then one can either leave the community (which might not be a pleasant alternative), or remain in the community and follow the standards (which might be unpleasant), or remain in the community and not follow the standards (which is often more unpleasant).

Before people have much input into community rule-making, they should have demonstrated, at least to some extent, their ability to understand and respect the rights of those in charge. To engage children in discussions about rules can be helpful, but the most important thing in this whole process is that they believe that someone cares about them who believes in their worth. This they perceive more through experiencing those who care about them and believe in their worth than by just talking.

Before exploring the justifications for rules, children first have to learn what living in a particular community is all about. Newcomers to any group, in my experience, first show respect for wherever they are and get used to the environment and the rules. One of the ways that encourages us to respect others is the guidance we get from the established rules, reflecting the beliefs and values of the community. The planning stage in the process discussed in this book teaches children to work things out within the structure of the organization. The planning sheets are very detailed. Figuring out a better way is the key. What guides us is our thinking. The child who breaks a rule probably feels justified—but could have solved the problem by thinking of a better way. Still, we *must* be primarily concerned about creating and maintaining right order wherever we are, so that everyone gets along.

5. Some might ask, "Your techniques seem to stress obedience, but isn't obedience really contrary to human nature, which rebels against authority?"

I think obedience is very much a part of human nature; not blind obedience, but obedience tied to love. Children generally follow the instructions of teachers they like, but they often have problems with teachers they dislike. Show me a classroom where there is order and harmony, and I'll show you a classroom, in nearly all cases, where the teacher is respected and liked.

This is also true for life in general. It is very hard to work for a supervisor you don't like or for whom you don't have respect; and most people will not only work hard, but "go the extra mile" for someone whom they like. When the head of the machinists' union at Southwest Airlines was asked how he got along with the company's Chief Executive Officer, his reply was classic: "Well, it's hard not to get along with someone who shows up at three o'clock in the morning with coffee and donuts and wants to chat about how things are going." The closer relationships are at home, the more likely children will do things for their parents, or spouses for each other. My wife Hester doesn't have to ask me to do much for her, because I want to please her and thus find myself looking for things to do that I know she wants done. That's just the way people who love each other act. My obedience comes not from my perceiving Hester as demanding or manipulative, but rather from my readiness to act on what she wants, a readiness born out of my love for my wife. Obedience has to come from love for control systems to get along with each other.

RTP is built to foster mutual respect. In contrast, those who demand that students comply do so without any thought of the relationship that is needed. In those cases, students will often rebel against authority, thus acting, in PCT terms, to cancel the disturbance.

6. Some might urge negotiation with children who are breaking rules: when a child breaks a rule, why not ask the child why he or she broke it?

In my experience, asking a child "why" leads directly to reasons, excuses, and avoidance of responsibility. If I had the child's trust, the child might actually tell me, "Because it's a stupid rule!" That would open the door to a discussion. "Why is it stupid?" "Do you know what the rule is for?" "Do you have a better idea?" "Would you like this rule better if you were me and I were you?" "Did this rule keep you from getting something you wanted?"

But to negotiate a rule with a child *when he is breaking the rule* doesn't make sense. His actions weren't what he was thinking about; as with Hunter in Chapter 2 of this book, the actions were merely the means to achieve his goal. Focusing on actions is starting at the wrong place. Asking "why" isn't going to tell you what he wanted, it is only going to get you an excuse to absolve him from the responsibility of respecting the rights of others. You need to tie the actions to the rules. Never give children a chance to excuse actions!

Also, never ask the child what she wants until she has first committed to following the rules, thus respecting the rights of others. Sometimes a child will use what she wanted as the excuse for her disruption. Once she has committed to following the rules, when she considers getting what she wants, it can be within the context of her being willing to maintain harmony in the community by following the rules.

Chapter 15
Thoughts from Educators Who Helped Implement This Discipline Program

Initially I worked with these people to establish a successful discipline program. Here are their thoughts on the program five months after we started.

—*Ed Ford*

George T. Venetis
Principal
Solano Elementary School
Osborn School District
Phoenix, Arizona

I strongly believe that the effectiveness of any model for school discipline reform depends on how well all of the components of that model are interwoven. Each part depends on the others, and all must work together to create a cohesive whole. The absence of even one part can render an entire program less effective.

A common scenario in education is to concentrate on training teachers and administrators to deal more effectively with problem children—almost as though these educators were the only ones who play a part in the child's educational journey. What about the child's first teacher—the parent? And what about the other members of the school community who come in contact with the child? The school secretary? Classroom aides? Bus drivers and cafeteria workers? Even substitute teachers? Doesn't it make sense to include every member of the school community in the discipline program?

At this point you might be wondering what kind of discipline program could benefit every member of the school community—a program that all can understand and use. And even if such a program were to be found, how would it be funded?

The answer to the first question came to me when I attended a presentation by Ed Ford, where he introduced his Home/School Discipline Program that provides both parents and school personnel with the tools for building strong relationships with their children and helps them to establish standards of discipline by teaching responsible thinking to children. In Ed's program, parents, teachers, and the rest of the school staff are no longer being put in the position of trying to control the behavior of their children. The focus of control is shifted to the child—where it belongs. The children are taught to think in a responsible manner, which eventually leads to their acting responsibly. How else can a child learn responsibility?

In my school district, this approach made sense not only to the parents, but to the entire school community. It was the answer we had been looking for. Every member of the school community could benefit. Ed had managed to concretize perceptual control theory into a process that is easy to understand and implement. His training techniques, which can be taught in one- or two-day sessions, enable participants to apply the process immediately. I knew at once that this was the program we needed. I began to wonder if parents and teachers would become as excited about this program as I had.

With my encouragement, Ed was invited by the Solano Elementary School Parent-Teachers Association to present his discipline program. This meeting proved to be the catalyst for bringing Ed back for further training. Parents and teachers stated loud and clear that this was a program that they wanted, and more importantly, would support. *BINGO!* We were off and running.

This eventually led to the second question: How could such a program be funded? The answer came sooner than I expected. Clarendon Elementary School joined Solano along with the Teachers' Education Association to undertake funding for the training in both schools. It literally became *our program*, and everyone in both schools made a commitment to develop and implement it. They demonstrated their commitment by attending Saturday training sessions without any remuneration whatsoever. Parents, teachers, administrators, all learning together!

The word soon spread throughout the school district. Parents and staff members began talking about the positive changes in children they had noticed both at home and at school. Everyone, without exception, reported being able to deal with children in a more relaxed way. No longer did they feel that they had to "control" children, and that they were responsible for the choices children made.

At school, children who continued to disrupt and who chose to infringe on the rights of others were removed from where they were not being successful and were being sent to the RTC. This classroom became the focal point of the school discipline program. It became the place where children were taught how to get along with others, how to make plans, and what respect for others is all about.

During the beginning stages of the program, we learned that it is critical to staff the RTC adequately. A certified teacher and an aide received training from Ed in this essential component of the program. The RTC staff worked hand-in-hand with students and classroom teachers to help children make better choices. The RTC teacher literally screened children, deciding how to work with them and their teachers, and determining which students needed to see an administrator or school psychologist. No longer were children crowding the school's office, waiting to see the principal. No longer were students sent back to the classroom because an administrator was not available. Students were prioritized as to their need to see the principal, and they were kept in the RTC until an administrator could meet with them.

During the first few months of the program, we also learned that it was vital for the school's administration to work closely with the RTC teacher. Initially, this room was flooded with a "tidal wave" of children—children who in the past had to be kept in the regular classrooms even though they continued to disrupt, because there was no place to send them, or because teachers were made to feel guilty or inadequate if they could not control the children. This initial influx of students lasted for about two months. Eventually, as students got used to our system and learned to think responsibly and make better choices, the number of students in the RTC diminished.

As I reflect on the first few months of our program, I realize that we got through that difficult period only by sticking to what we believed in and working together, knowing that this was the kind of struggle that must be endured: the journey through the process where meaningful learning takes place.

A final note with regard to the school administration. School administrators need to have a vision of the *entire* program. School community members have only partial views, based on their more limited and individual roles. Administrators need to be aware of how each role affects the total picture. When a change is made in one area, it is essential to assess this change to see what effect it has on the entire process and to make sure that what has changed is aligned and consistent with what we know and what we believe. It is critical that this vision eventually become the vision of the building core team. This will insure the integrity and the continuance of the program when district and building administrators move to other jobs or locations.

Finally, I would like to give special recognition to a very special person and a very special friend—LeEdna Custer-Knight, Clarendon School psychologist. She was instrumental in the initial implementation of Ed's program. We shared our vision together through the rough waters of change, and with the cooperation of everyone, we made it happen.

LeEdna Custer-Knight
School Psychologist
Clarendon Elementary School
Osborn School District
Phoenix, Arizona

Current trends in education have resulted in significant changes in the role of the school psychologist. We have moved from the psycho-medical role of diagnosis and placement of "problem children," which usually resulted in little or no interaction with "regular students," to more inclusive methods of intervention. Currently, we're working with more and more children in the regular classroom. This, plus the ever-growing numbers of children entering our schools with limited social skills, has created a tremendous need for a simple, logical, and non-punitive discipline program to insure that teachers can teach and students can learn.

Never before had I felt this need more acutely than last fall. We began the school year with 13 new teachers out of a total of 36. Given that we are a multicultural inner-city school with a highly transitory population, a significant number of our families living in poverty, and an ever-growing problem of youth gangs, the addition of a large influx of new, inexperienced teachers resulted in an overwhelming need for an effective school-wide discipline program. George Venetis and I had heard Ed Ford speak the year before and believed that his approach was the answer to our school's discipline problems. However, funding from the district was not forthcoming. One year later, we found ourselves in even greater need. George approached the Parent-Teachers Association for funding, and I approached the staff. I asked them to give up two Saturdays to participate in Ed's training with no pay. To our delight, both groups said yes, and the teachers' union added to the PTA funding of the project. We were off. After the initial training, we began a multi-year commitment as a staff to work together to create responsible thinking in our students.

We are now almost at the end of our first year, and the overall changes in students are amazing. Teachers support the program 100%. Parents who have participated in the training understand the program, support the school, and use the same methods to deal with their children at home. Students have a clear understanding that they have choices and are responsible for their decisions, including the resulting consequences.

What role did I as school psychologist play in the development of a strong school-wide responsible thinking program? I tried to be an innovator, bringing information, credibility, and motivation to the staff. I found that I needed to be committed to a greater depth of training. Once we had learned the techniques, George and I assisted Ed in the training of staff and parents. It is critical that as the psychologist, I should be considered "expert" on and in alignment with the program, the skills required, and the process of program development. Teachers and parents need key personnel who can solve problems in difficult cases. I felt that I had to satisfy that role.

The psychologist should be a critical member of the core team developing and sustaining the program and its developmental process. This includes nurturing the RTC, establishing the room's guidelines and procedures, creating standards for classroom and school-wide rules, and ultimately determining the procedures for removal and processing of disruptive students. Additionally, I had to make myself available to go through the questioning process with the most difficult students, and I had to commit to developing relationships with these students.

The psychologist has to be a role model of the process at its best. I had to facilitate class discussions as a way of modeling appropriate practices for classroom teachers, which also provided me with the true experience of dealing with large groups of children in the regular classroom, lest I ever be tempted to forget the tremendous job required of the classroom teacher each day. This also allowed me to provide support for teachers whose skills had not developed sufficiently to meet the challenges of the classroom.

The most difficult task of implementing this program was not, as some might suspect, getting teachers to commit their free weekend time to the necessary training for skills development, nor getting everyone to "buy into" the responsible thinking program itself, nor getting commitment to school-wide rules. Rather, the toughest part of the program lay in the day-to-day operation of the school as the program took shape and form, as our attitudes toward each other began to change. The attitude changes happened in all of us, teachers, administrators, school support staff, parents, and, more importantly, the students themselves. It has been a significant transformation in how we look at ourselves, and at each other, especially our children.

The daily struggles were in:

• keeping a large group of people and procedures aligned.

• making written copies of all rules, procedures, and changes in forms available to all staff, students, and parents.

• accepting the fact that initial discipline referrals were going to increase in number until students learned that this process was consistently in place and here to stay.

• empowering staff to take responsibility to quickly and professionally address concerns through the core team.

• knowing how and when to confront issues of non-aligned behavior in staff at every level.

• ensuring that enough staff members were highly skilled in the program so that the loss of a few key people did not cripple the program.

• exhibiting personal vigilance and always adhering to the process.

• renewing our commitment to responsible thinking as a staff on a regular basis.

• continuing to talk, talk, talk, realizing that earnest dialogue concerning the success as well as the difficulties of all staff are critical to the maintenance and growth of the program.

Darleen Martin
Responsible Thinking Classroom Teacher
Clarendon Elementary School
Osborn School District
Phoenix, Arizona

The RTC is the place where disruptive children go when they infringe on the rights of others, and the place where students can calm down and collect themselves. Serious acts of misconduct, such as "assault with intent to commit bodily harm," are mandated by district policy for out-of-school suspension. We deal with all other kinds of problems in the RTC.

Students choose to leave their classrooms for disrespect, disruption, or disobedience. The students report to the RTC during the time they are normally with the teacher who is in charge of where they chose to leave; they attend their other regular classes. In order to be re-admitted to the class where there were problems, the students must negotiate with the person in charge of where they chose to leave. I've found that it is critical for the staff to be consistent about the requirement for negotiating a student's return. To ensure student success, the staff must not deviate from a student's plan once the teacher and the student have agreed to a plan. During negotiations, teachers are encouraged to change those parts of plans with which they disagree. But once a plan is set, it should be followed.

Also, it is critical that there be consistency with regard to the clear-cut definition of terms. In our school, terms such as "assault," "fighting," and "reckless horseplay" needed to be clearly defined so that all teachers used the same meanings. The teachers had to become more specific when explaining exactly what had happened in incidents. The more specific they were in explaining what had occurred, the easier it was to work with the students, especially when it came to helping them create workable plans.

At the start of a normal day, students begin arriving at the RTC after first checking in with their homeroom teachers for attendance. As they arrive, we determine which classes they are permitted to attend. During the time that they are with us, when they are ready, we teach them how to develop plans, discussing alternative, acceptable choices when future problems arise. During the day, students are constantly arriving or leaving for classes, so we have to keep track of who needs to be where, and when. This takes a lot of organizing, requiring from teachers each student's schedule, including special classes for some students.

Timing is very important. Teachers can be contacted by students who want to negotiate only at certain times to avoid disrupting a class during instruction time. A student's lack of concern about disrupting a class when she re-enters her class displays her lack of willingness to accept class rules.

When our room gets overloaded with students, where they sit depends on how easily they can communicate or entertain one another. At those times, the job is mainly one of monitoring behavior as opposed to working one-on-one with students, teaching them how to make plans. Students are served lunch in our room, are escorted on any restroom breaks, and are given passes to attend classes.

When children have returned and have been re-admitted to classes, teachers often seat them at desks separated from the other students until they can demonstrate responsibility. I've found that the entire school staff now works more effectively toward helping the child succeed in the classroom.

Each child's situation must be assessed on an individual basis, thus creative counseling is the key to teaching responsible thinking. For example, a young boy, age 13, returned from a district-mandated out-of-school suspension for fighting. While Ed and I were working on his plan with him, we came up with "the buddy plan," in which a close friend helps him refrain from getting into fights. He also elected to come to the RTC to "chill out" when his anger began to get the best of him, regardless of where he was at the time. It's been a month now, and I've only seen the student once; that was to "chill out." For many children, name-calling and put-downs are a way of life and often lead to fights. This is where "social skills" really need to be taught.

There were times when I thought certain students were making their plans with certain choices simply to get back to class. But I've watched many children begin to think for themselves, to act more responsibly. They've learned to think: "If I act a certain way, will it get me what I really want?" When we began this program, we were overwhelmed with children. At times, it got discouraging. But as the children got used to the process, and as teachers, administrators, parents, and counselors began to see our value and to work more closely with us, things began to change. It was as if everyone who was part of the process began to catch on to what Ed's program is all about at the same time. Now there are fewer children coming to our room—mostly the chronically disruptive children, to whom we can give lots of time, doing all we can to help them succeed.

There are so many success stories. One student had a hard time getting from her home room to her special education class. She often was found playing tetherball. When I worked with her on developing a plan, we decided that she would walk to her class via another route. She now comes past my room and through the courtyard area to her class. This way, she completely avoids the playground area and the temptations of the tetherball courts. The most recent example happened on a Monday morning on the baseball field, prior to the beginning of school. Two sixth grade boys began arguing, and soon fists began to fly. In the past, a large crowd would gather, and onlookers would "feed" the situation, encouraging the fight. This morning was different. Three of their classmates pulled the boys apart and stopped the fighting. Now, that has never happened before. That's what responsible thinking is all about.

Part 2. Practical Advice

Chapter 16
How Did We Do It?

Ed Snyder
Principal
Boyne City Elementary School
Boyne City, Michigan

and

Wendy Thomas
Social Worker
Boyne City Elementary School
Boyne City, Michigan

Boyne City Elementary School has experienced a seven-year journey from a stimulus-response school to a responsible thinking process school. The first question that visitors to our school ask us is, "How did you do it?"—which really translates into, "How can *we* do it?" We have thought about this question many times and feel that the answer lies in the outcomes of our past struggles and in what we have discovered along the way.

We have discovered that any school interested in such a change should address the following:

1. *Articulate a need.* Staff and students must define the need for a change and ask the question, "Is what we are doing getting us what we want?" If the answer is "no," then there must be a better way.

2. *Create a vision.* Don't be afraid to dream of the best school that could possibly exist. Share the vision with all players and model the vision.

3. *Form a psychological premise based on best knowledge and practice.* Do your homework! It is here that you

will need research to enhance and "prove" your beliefs and strategies.

4. *Establish expectations for the way people—parents, students, staff, and visitors—will be treated in your learning community.* Agree on how to treat each other and give permission for people to settle disagreements and solve problems in a professional manner.

5. *Train staff.* Have resources and opportunities for training all staff in both RTP and PCT. It is important that every person have the knowledge to be "in the same book," even if everyone is not "on the same page." Remember, some individuals have a great deal of difficulty accepting change.

6. *Develop a realistic timeline for implementation.* Keep the purpose of change in the forefront, but move forward in an ordered and consistent manner. Remember your vision.

7. *Re-visit, evaluate, and adjust—continually monitor your program for both problems and successes.* Keep good records and redefine problem areas whenever necessary. Fine-tune your program and keep all staff updated on results.

8. *Celebrate success!* Change is hard work. Don't forget to celebrate the positive outcomes as you are working on the problem areas. Every once in a while, take a look back to see just how far you have come.

Our Demographics

Boyne City Elementary is a K–4 building with 500 students located in northwest lower Michigan. There are 30 certified staff and 31 non-certified staff. We have a diverse student population, with the majority being in low- to middle-income-level households. We have a 27% transient rate, 30% of students receive free or reduced-price lunch, and 11% are in special education.

Why We Needed to Change

Once it became clear to us, through increasing numbers of discipline referrals and increasing severity of referrals, that what we were doing was not getting us what we wanted, we knew it was time for a change. Prior to 1991, we were a stimulus-response school, with rules posted, student names on the boards with checks, and so on. The end result of our disciplinary process was a trip to the principal's office—as if the "big guy" could make students do what they needed to do. It was obvious that this did not work for our students, and morale was down. Through careful dialog, the staff began to see a need for a different way to deal with discipline in our school. Deciding what this "new" program would look like was the problem. We first had to create a vision of what could be!

Our Vision

We began our new program based on the theory that the purpose of discipline is to *teach*. The following beliefs illustrate the requirements we set for a good discipline program.

• We should send each child home happy every day.

• No decision is made that intentionally could harm a child.

• No child is permitted to interrupt the education of other children.

• No child is permitted to threaten the safety of other children.

• Self-esteem comes from success and is important to everyone at school.

• Discipline should be a learning experience.

• Students can be taught to make good choices and accept responsibility for their behavior.

• Staff must be able to model the behavior expected from students.

Our Search for a Solution

In 1990, our entire staff was trained in a social skills program. This program was then taught in every classroom. The students were presented with ideas about how to act in various situations. We used these skills as frameworks for administering discipline. This worked for some students, but it did not teach students to take responsibility for their behavior. In 1992, our district became involved with the ODDM movement. At that time, we started what we term our "first-generation" RTC. We didn't yet have a well-developed underlying theory, but we saw the need for a non-threatening place for students to go where they could feel secure, discuss problems, and avoid disrupting classrooms.

Developing Our Psychological Base

As we explored different ideas, we knew that we had to change the perception of some staff that discipline equals punishment. We worked closely with John Champlin, and we heard Ed Ford speak about RTP and PCT. Our district sent key staff to an Ed Ford in-service. Following that in-service, the staff felt that Ed Ford's explanation of the responsible thinking process and perceptual control theory, and the questions he asked of students, were the psychological pieces we had been missing.

What We Needed to Change

As our staff discussed RTP and PCT, we determined that each of us needed to understand what it would mean to change and how change would affect the following areas:

Culture: How we act within the organization.

Climate: How people act toward each other in the school.

Trust: Doing what we say we will do.

Decision-making processes: Changing from a top-down to a consensus school.

What Needed to Be in Place before Implementation

As soon as we made the decision to embrace RTP, we worked hard to have the following things in place:
- Board of Education support.
- Central office support.
- Parent support.
- Financial resources.
- Training for the entire staff.
- Policy and procedures for the RTC.
- Classroom space.
- Personnel to staff the RTC.

How We Have Maintained the Program

This is the third year of our RTC. We try constantly to keep the program a priority of our school. We discuss, report, and share with staff, students, and parents whenever possible. We continue to teach responsible thinking skills in every classroom. We provide an orientation for all students in kindergarten and first grade. We provide all new kindergarten parents with a tour of the RTC and discuss RTP strategies for use at home. A school success team consisting of the principal, social worker, at-risk coordinator, special education teachers, and RTC staff was formed. This team meets every Friday to discuss individual students and to review RTC data and strategies. Finally, we model the behavior we want to see from students so that all see it is a priority.

Staff Comments

When our staff was asked what we should say to other schools interested in making the change from a stimulus-response school to an RTP school, here are some of things they said:
- "Give it time to work."
- "Be prepared for K–1 to be the busiest."

• "Make policy clear to parents."
• "It really has eliminated confrontation."
• "It takes the teacher out of the power struggle with students."
• "This lets kids learn."
• "There are now minimal disruptions in the classroom."
• "Try hard as a staff to define who comes and what for—then stick to it."
• "I like the idea that students leave the room and don't feel they are being punished."
• "When students return to the room they are ready to learn."

Hard Evidence: It Works!

We continually look for evidence that our discipline program is doing what we want it to do. It is important to know if we are true to our vision of what is good for students. We have determined that the following have happened:

• Referrals to the principal for discipline have dropped dramatically.
• The principal now spends less than 5% of his time on discipline, not 50%, as in the past.
• Absentee rates of staff have dropped.
• There is very little negative contact with parents.
• There is an observable improvement in student behavior.
• Climate and environment have improved, as measured by comments from visitors in the building.

Final Thoughts

If teachers have a student who needs help in reading or math, they think nothing of referring that student for extra help. We need to apply the same thought process to students who need help with behavior. We have to provide the opportunity and teach the students the appropriate behavior skills, just as if they had an academic problem. When a student visits the RTC, we ask parents to encourage responsible thinking by asking their child, "What did you learn?" or "What will you do differently next time?"

This program works, and it is right for kids!

Chapter 17
Thoughts and Suggestions
from an RTC Teacher

Darleen Martin
RTC Teacher
Clarendon Elementary School
Osborn School District
Phoenix, Arizona

Darleen Martin is the first RTC teacher. I worked with her as I created the RTC, and she has been helping me improve on the original model ever since. She is among the best, and many other RTC teachers have spent hours learning from this highly skilled and competent teacher.

—*Ed Ford*

In December 1993, my principal offered me the opportunity to be our school's first responsible thinking classroom teacher. I excitedly accepted the challenge. RTP's logical approach to helping students think for themselves to resolve their difficulties captured me! Although I've had three opportunities to teach in a regular classroom, I've chosen to stay in the RTC. Rebecca McNany, my aide, who has been with the program since its birth, has also chosen to stay.

I have often been asked, "How can you do this day after day, and year after year?" I guess it's those everyday little miracles. Take Eddie, for instance. In the 4th grade, he was disruptive and volatile. During the 5th grade, he became very explosive, and we spent a great deal of time working on anger management. Last September, Eddie returned as a 6th grader and was given the following assignment: "Have you or someone you know ever worked hard to achieve a difficult goal? Write a paragraph discussing this goal." Here is his paragraph:

> Last year I had the worst temper in the world. If anyone would say anything wrong to me I would start throwing objects in the classroom. One time by accident I almost hit a group of people. But as the year went on I had gotten control of my temper and that was very important to me. Another thing that was sorta important to me is when the RTC teacher asked me that if I had any spare time to help a little boy in the fourth grade who had the same problem I did earlier in the school year. My goals were to help the little boy and help myself.

After Eddie had developed some self-control while in the 5th grade, I had asked him to talk with Breen, a 4th grade student who was displaying similar actions to those Eddie displayed the year before. I have found that by pairing students or by arranging for mentors, two results often happen: the student having difficulties is receptive to input from a peer who has experienced the same difficulties, and the peer or mentor further builds his self-esteem and continues to be successful.

Typically a shy boy, Eddie voluntarily read his paragraph to the class and bashfully gave permission to reprint it here. I thank his teacher, Joyce Merritt, for sharing this with me. There are many, many stories similar to Eddie's that I could tell.

A recurring question I've heard over the years from classroom teachers is "How do I keep track of which students have disrupted and how many times?" One 5th grade teacher developed an easy method. She simply had a copy of the daily attendance record nearby and placed a checkmark by the name of each student she had to ask, "What are you doing?", "What are the rules?", etc. Thus, she just referred to the list when a disturbance occurred, and if the disruptive student had a previous checkmark, then that student had chosen to go to the RTC. At the end of each day, the class began to tally how many disruptions occurred that day. They then set goals for fewer interruptions the next day. Soon, students began to graph the number of disruptions and figure percentages. The teacher incorporated this into their math lessons. This example is from a teacher who admittedly did not use RTP during the previous two years!

Another teacher concern is the classroom instruction that a student misses because he is in the RTC. In reply, I pose two questions. First, "Is the student learning when he is disrupting?" Second, "Are the other students in the classroom learning when the student is disrupting?" Through discussions of this nature, teachers realize that once the student causing difficulties is removed, the class can continue learning. The student who has chosen to go to the RTC, with guidance, can realize what it is he wants and how to get what he wants without infringing on the rights of others.

A particular situation I am thinking of involved a 5th grade student whom I had only seen sporadically until the month of February. In February, Domiano became a "frequent flyer." His teacher and I sat down and brainstormed about what he was controlling for. His teacher expressed concern about how far behind Domiano was. This was out of character for this bright young man. While talking with Domiano, I realized that he knew he was behind in his classes and wanted to do something about it but didn't know how. He felt as though there was no light at the end of the tunnel! His mother had started a new job in January which required her to leave for work before Domiano came home from school. She usually was asleep when he got ready for school in the mornings, so they were seeing each other less frequently. The plan that Domiano developed and negotiated with his teacher stated that he would come to me each morning and at the end of each day to discuss completed work and what he would take home to do each evening. With a slight amount of acknowledgement and someone with whom to share his accomplishments, Domi-ano became caught up in his school work.

It is imperative that there be open dialogue between the RTC teacher and other staff. A good time to meet with staff is when they have grade-level meetings. The groups are smaller, and specific concerns can be addressed. In my school, there are certain student restrooms for each grade level. A great increase in graffiti became noticeable in the 6th grade boys' restroom. The problem was discussed at a grade-level meeting, and the teachers agreed to keep sign-out sheets for students using the restroom. During the day, staff checked the restroom, noting the time and amount of graffiti. By comparing the sign-out sheets with the teachers' notes, we were able to determine who was responsible. Through this cooperative effort, we were able to minimize the gang writing and restore a feeling of safety and pride to the school.

Sometimes, instead of trying to explain how to overcome an objection, I simply role-play with the teacher. This has proved to be invaluable. By modeling the situation, you provide a clearer understanding for the teacher and an opportunity to discuss pitfalls to avoid.

A solid, strong working relationship is important not only between the RTC teacher and staff, but also between the RTC teacher and administrators. An important factor in the success of the RTC is that the administrators remain approachable and supportive. Never have I felt threatened or intimidated when a disagreement occurs. These situa-tions have been resolved through discussion, with valuable input from all involved. Nor have I been made to feel un-comfortable for any decisions I've made. I have been in numerous conferences with administrators, staff, students, and parents. It still amazes me how the questioning process enlightens the irate parent about the circumstances sur-rounding the purpose of the conference. There have been times when a parent has come in furious with me for un-justly sending her child home. During the conference, the parent realizes that the child has caused a disturbance at least four times before losing the privilege of remaining at school for the rest of the day. When a student has to go home from the RTC because of his disruptions, it is the administrator who transports that student if a parent is unable to come for the student. Needing to take a student home often occurs at an inopportune time, making administrative commitment crucial. The re-entry process the next day requires a conference involving a parent, the student, an administrator, and myself. During the conference, the student's commitment and his willingness to work on returning to the classroom are discussed. He remains at school, starting in the RTC.

Conferences with students and parents are extremely revealing. Many times I have heard, "It's the school's fault," "another student started it," "another student did it too, and he wasn't sent home." One father told his son to "hold onto your anger, because anger is power!" The key to a successful conference with an upset parent is to remember to ask questions of not only the student but the parent as well. What is it that the parent wants for her child, and what does the child want? How can we work together to attain that?

This brings to mind the following incident. I walked into the principal's office to overhear an irate mother expressing to the assistant principal that I had not taken care of an incident the previous day. Her 4th grade son had told her that he was beaten up after school by a 6th grade boy. Furthermore, she said that I had threatened to call the police to arrest her son. The mother was so upset with me that initially she would not even acknowledge my presence. After she had finished explaining the situation as she knew it, I asked her if she would mind if I asked her son, Lawson, some questions. Hesitantly, she shrugged her shoulders and nodded permission. I then asked Lawson if I could ask him some questions. (Note that both parent and student were asked for permission.) The first question I asked Lawson was "Did I call you to the RTC yesterday so we could talk about what happened?" Lawson answered, "Yes." "Did I also discuss what happened with Nelson and Preston?"

"Yes." "Did I talk to each of you separately, then all together?" "Yes." "How did everyone agree this happened?" "An accident when we were playing basketball." At this time, in amazement, Lawson's mother said, "Playing basketball—you didn't tell me that. I thought he was picking on you!" Next I asked Lawson, "What solution did the three boys decide on yesterday?" The agreement was that the 4th graders would play basketball only with 4th graders, and the 6th graders would play basketball only with 6th graders.

Next, we addressed the issue of the police, again through a questioning process. (Lawson had come to the RTC on a time-out and, while in the RTC, decided that he wanted to go home. Since there was no phone at his home, and an administrator who could transport him was at lunch, I explained to Lawson that he would have to wait a few minutes. Lawson then said that he would walk home, and that I couldn't stop him.) As Lawson's mother repositioned herself in her chair so that she could better see Lawson, I asked, "Did you tell your mother I was going to call the police on you?" Lawson answered, "Yes." "Did you tell your mother what you told me you were going to do?" "No." Lawson's mother asked, "Lawson, what were you going to do?" "Walk home." I asked, "Lawson, did you and I have a conversation about what the law requires me to do if you leave campus by yourself?" "Yes." "Did you explain this to your mother?" Lawson's mother interjected, "No, he certainly did not! I walk in here today, mad, thinking he's being intimidated by a 6th grader, and that you were threatening to call the police. This certainly is turning out differently from what I heard at home, and I am really, really sorry. Son, you and I have some things to discuss this evening!"

At the beginning of the school year, all teachers bring their classes to the RTC for 20-minute orientation sessions. These sessions serve as refreshers for former students and staff and as introductions for all new members of the student body and staff to RTC policies, procedures, and purposes. The students can experience how the RTC looks and feels, and how a student can begin to resolve her problems. I go over making plans with them, role-play, and answer questions. The students begin to perceive the RTC as a problem-solving room. It's important that children learn to make a safe world for themselves. They need to think through and then implement successful ways of handling situations. The plan-making process helps develop a helpful pattern of thought.

This brings to mind a 4th grade student, Patrick, who at the beginning of the school year came to the RTC for slapping another student. This had been witnessed by the classroom teacher. He came in, got a plan, and sat and sat. I went over to him a few times, asked what he had done, what his teacher saw him do, and tried to guide him into accepting responsibility for his actions and working on a plan. His repeated reply was "I didn't do anything." After a period of time, I approached him again and asked, "Patrick, what did your hands do?" His reply was, "Oh," and he began to work on his plan. Instead of me telling him what his teacher said he did, he accepted responsibility for his actions once the right question was asked.

In order for the RTC teacher to be able to ask the right questions and effectively help a student develop a plan, it is imperative that there be a brief description on the referral form (shown at the end of this chapter), as opposed to just a checkmark describing the infraction. In other words, what specifically did the student do (talking out, wandering around the room, flicking paper across the desk)?

Once the student has written an acceptable plan and we have reviewed it together, I contact the classroom teacher for a conference time so that the student can negotiate his return to class. Teachers must keep in mind the meaning of "negotiate"—attempting to reach a mutual agreement—so as to guarantee discussion with the goal of arriving at a settlement. View such negotiations as quality time. If a teacher feels that the student's commitment is not genuine, or that there is a lack of sincerity during the negotiation process, then the student should return to the RTC to review what it is that he wants. (An error only becomes a mistake when you refuse to fix it!) The teacher and student can agree to changes made in the plan.

With the assistance of the school psychologist, we've been able to recognize behavior patterns when we've reviewed the referrals. For example, one student was coming to the RTC from various classes between 10:30 and 11:30 a.m. By changing the time he took his morning medication, he greatly reduced his classroom disruptions. In the beginning of the year, Haley was one of our "frequent flyers." She was constantly getting out of her seat. We tried various interventions. Her plans included taping a note on her desk to remind herself to stay seated, monitor sheets, and placing her desk next to the teacher's. Haley still continued to jump out of her seat without thinking. I suggested that she take off one shoe when she was supposed to work at her desk. This would provide a cue to her that something was amiss when she stood up—she could feel that the shoe was off. She incorporated my suggestion into her plan. In a short time, Haley was able to stay seated at her desk with both shoes on. Be creative and think "outside the lines"!

The physical layout of the RTC is an important factor. The RTC at my school has four carrels consisting of two seating stations each. Becky McNany and I sit diagonally across the room, allowing a clear view of all students. Individual desks are placed in the center and around the perimeter of the room to provide additional seating. Next to my desk are two small rooms containing a single desk, chair, and a door (with a window) that a student can close should he want privacy. These "cubbies" are used by any student who chooses to go to a safe, quiet place. Having a "chill-out" place for students to go to re-group and collect themselves has been quite effective. This is especially true for those dealing with a highly volatile temper. Once calmed down, they can return to the classroom whenever they choose. It helps the students to have a place to stop and think about what is happening, and about what choices they need to make in order to remain successful. So as not to distract others, students are asked to remain seated, facing forward, at all times. Students can develop a plan to solve their problems, read, rest their heads on their desks, do schoolwork, or just sit and think. They must remain seated and quiet. Originally, Becky and I would escort the students as a group to the restroom twice daily, in the morning and afternoon. Now students sign an in-and-out time sheet. This change was successful with all but four students; it remained necessary to escort them.

The responsibilities of Rebecca McNany, my RTC aide, include, but are not limited to, the following: 1. Assisting in maintaining an orderly, quiet, problem-solving environment. 2. Maintaining a daily log of student names, entry times, and infractions, and accurate accounts of all pertinent information. 3. Ensuring that students are supervised at all times. 4. Performing all clerical duties. The RTC aide must have the ability to support the concept of responsible thinking; effectively communicate with students, parents, and staff; and support the overall RTC climate. Becky does an outstanding job.

There are three *musts* for the staff if the RTC is to function properly: commitment, consistency, and dedication to listening and asking questions. This is a team effort, and each player is a valuable component of the program.

I would like to leave you with one final story. It was the day before Christmas break. Two 6th grade boys came to the RTC with a very special Christmas gift. Since they had limited funds for Christmas spending, they decided to "do" something for Mrs. McNany and me in the true spirit of giving. They announced that they were going to clean the room so it would be fresh when we returned from the holiday break. They proceeded to scrub the desks, straighten books, remove old tape, replace forms that needed replenishing, and so forth. Two years earlier, one of those 6th grade boys had been running with a gang, was arrested for breaking and entering, and was obviously headed down the wrong course. Another of the many miracles I see as an RTC teacher!

RESPONSIBLE THINKING CLASSROOM REFERRAL FORM

Student _____

Only short phrases are necessary ...

1. Briefly describe the first disruption (please be
   specific).

   _____

   _____

   _____

2. Briefly describe the next disruption that resulted
   in the student choosing to go to the RTC.

   _____

   _____

   _____

3. Additional violation of school rules, student comments
   and/or behaviors during or after the disruption.

   _____

   _____

   _____

   _____

Referring Teacher_____

Date _____ Period _____ Time Sent _____

Chapter 18
Dealing with Students
Who've Been Fighting

George Venetis
Principal
Solano Elementary School
Osborn School District
Phoenix, Arizona

To help the reader understand how the RTP questioning process works, in this chapter are sample discussions similar to those I have had with many students. A word of caution, however. The following discussions are much longer than is typical. What I've done is to include several questioning techniques to show the various ways of dealing with students. In a school that has been using RTP for some time, working with students generally goes much more quickly. The reason for this is that students become familiar with the questioning process; rarely do they offer excuses. Instead, they focus on solving their problems. I once had a visiting principal watch me work with several students, one of whom was new to the school. I asked the visitor if he could identify the new student. The principal laughed and said, "That's easy, it was the one who insisted on giving numerous excuses."

The following discussions involve two students. The first student, whom I'll call Christian, has just hit another student, Brandt, in the face while they were playing basketball. Christian refuses to leave the playground and to go to the RTC. An administrator is called to the scene.

Administrator: Christian, you'll need to come with me to my office.

Christian: (No response.)

Administrator: Christian, if you don't come with me, what do you think will happen? (Remember to always ask questions in a calm, relaxed manner.)

Christian: (No response.)

Administrator: Christian, we'll have to call your parents, and if they can't be located or refuse to come, then we'll have to call the police. Is that what you want?

Christian: I don't care.

Administrator: Do you think not caring and our having to call your parents will make things better or worse for you?

(The main goal of the administrator is to get the child to commit to leaving the playground or classroom, wherever they're refusing to leave. At this point in time, the administrator leaves the teacher in charge and goes to call the parents or the police. As he leaves, he says, "I see you've chosen to have me call your parents or the police." Because the custom of the school has been firmly established, the student believes the administrator. The student is still in control, and his decisions are being respected. Most students will go with the administrator at that time. If they don't, then the parents are called. If the administrator backs down, the integrity of the program has been seriously compromised.

Christian is still mad and upset, but follows the administrator to the office without saying anything.)

Administrator (in his office with Christian): Christian, I see you're upset. Do you want to work at solving your problem now, or do you want to go to the RTC to calm down, and we can talk later? (Usually, most students will begin to tell the administrator what happened.)

Christian: He hit me first. And he's been making fun of me.

Administrator: Who hit you and teased you?

Christian: Brandt.

Administrator: Then what did you do?

Christian: I hit him back. My Dad told me I could defend myself if someone hit me. (I never criticize what parents have been reported as saying, rather I keep the student focused on the rules of where he is, namely in school.)

Administrator: What's the rule about hitting people here at school?

Christian: You're not allowed to hit others, and you're supposed to keep your hands and feet to yourself. But he hit me first. What's going to happen to *him*?

Administrator: Well, I'll talk with Brandt next. But Christian, who is it *you* control? (Many times students will divert attention to the other party involved. Remember, always keep them focused on who they control.)

Christian: Me.

Administrator: Then who is responsible for what *you* do?

Christian: I am.

Administrator: What happens when you hit someone at school?

Christian: I get in trouble.

Administrator: What do you mean, get in trouble? (I'm trying to get Christian to think in specific terms.)

Christian: I have to go to the RTC, and I could be suspended from school.

Administrator: Is that what you want?

Christian: No, but what do I do? Whenever I play basketball, he laughs at me when I miss a shot and tells my teammates that they're stupid for picking me to be on their team.

Administrator: Do you think that hitting Brandt will stop him from teasing and hitting you?

Christian: No.

Administrator: When you hit other students, do you get into trouble?

Christian: Yes.

Administrator: Is that what you want?

Christian: No.

Administrator: What are you going to do the next time Brandt teases or hits you?

Christian: I don't know.

Administrator: Do you want to continue to get into trouble?

Christian: No. But what about Brandt?

Administrator: With whom am I talking right now? (Many key questions have to be repeated, often with different phrasing, to assure that the student stays focused on the person over whom he has control, himself.)

Christian: Me.

Administrator: Are you willing to take responsibility for what you do and solve your problem?

Christian: I guess so.

Administrator (suspecting a weak commitment): Are you serious about this or not?

Christian: Yes.

Administrator: What are you going to do the next time Brandt teases and hits you?

Christian: I really don't know. Nothing seems to work.

Administrator: If I showed you a way to solve your problem and not get into trouble, would you be interested?

Christian: Yes.

Administrator: OK, what I'd like you to do is go to the RTC and work on a plan. Ms. Johnson is there if you need help. Meanwhile, I'm going to talk with Brandt. When I finish talking to Brandt, I'll bring both of you together and help you and Brandt work out a solution to your problem so that both of you don't continue to get into trouble. Christian, how does that sound?

Christian: OK.

(The administrator takes Christian to the RTC, where he can work with Nola Johnson, the RTC teacher. She will help him write a plan which should include how he is going to deal with the same or similar problem the next time it occurs. Meanwhile, Brandt is called in by the administrator, who will talk with him to find out what his perception of the problem is, and whether he is willing to resolve his conflict with Christian.)

Administrator: Brandt, what happened between you and Christian on the playground?

Brandt: We were playing basketball, and Christian told me to shut up, and then he pushed me.

Administrator: What were you saying to Christian when he told you to shut up?

Brandt: Nothing, I didn't do anything to him.

Administrator: What would Christian say you were doing?

Brandt: I don't know, he usually lies anyway.

Administrator: Christian said you were teasing him and making fun of him. He said that every time he missed a shot, you laughed and told the other players that they were stupid for having him on their team.

Brandt: Christian will say anything not to get into trouble.

Administrator: What would you think the other players on the teams would say?

Brandt: I don't know.

Administrator: Brandt, do you want to work at solving this problem or not? (If the student continues to deny any wrongdoing, then I send him to the RTC, since he is choosing not to work with me, and I call in witnesses to the incident to determine what has happened.)

Brandt: I was just playing around, and besides, that's no reason for him to hit me.

Administrator: What does playing around mean? (Again, I try to get the student to be specific; "playing around" doesn't say what he was doing.)

Brandt: I was just teasing him about missing so many shots. Then he said shut up and pushed me.

Administrator: After he said shut up and pushed you, then what did you do?

Brandt: I told him to stop pushing me, and he laughed at me, so I pushed him back.

Administrator: Is pushing and teasing allowed at school?

Brandt: No, but he pushed me first.

Administrator: Is pushing and teasing allowed at school? (When they answer the question but include an excuse, you ask the question again.)

Brandt: No.

Administrator: So, what happened when you pushed him back?

Brandt: He hit me in the face.

Administrator: Then what happened?

Brandt: The teacher came over and asked him what he just did. He wouldn't answer, so they called you.

Administrator: Do you think pushing Christian back helped solve the problem?

Brandt: No. But what could I do? He pushed me first. And besides, he pushes me every time we play basketball.

Administrator: Did you tell the teacher on duty about the problem?

Brandt: No, because she would just tell me to stay away from him, and then I wouldn't be able to play basketball if Christian was playing.

Administrator: What else can you do to solve the problem?

Brandt (showing frustration): I don't know.

Administrator: Well, did pushing him make things better or worse for you?

Brandt: Worse, he hit me in the face.

Administrator: Do you think that both of you will be allowed to play basketball if you continue teasing, pushing, and hitting each other?

Brandt: No. I'll leave him alone if he leaves me alone. (Any time a student uses the actions of another as a reason for what he does, then his move toward lack of responsibility has to be addressed.)

Administrator: Who controls what you do, you or Christian? (I refocus him on who is responsible for his actions.)

Brandt: I do.

Administrator: Would you like to find a way to solve the problem between you and Christian, so that you will be able to continue to play basketball during recess?

Brandt: Yes, if he will stop pushing and hitting me. (Brandt was making his future actions contingent on what Christian did, which is avoiding responsibility.)

Administrator: Would you like to find a way to solve the problem? (The key here is that if an excuse for actions is given, and the question really isn't answered, then you ask it again.)

Brandt: I guess. (Never accept a weak commitment from a student.)

Administrator: Are you really serious about wanting to work things out so that you can continue to play basketball?

Brandt: Yes, I just want to play basketball.

Administrator: Should we bring Christian in to see if the two of you can solve this problem?

Brandt: I don't care. (Again, a weak commitment.)

Administrator: Do you really want to solve this problem or not?

Brandt: I guess I do. (Still another weak commitment.)

Administrator: How will you solve the conflict if the two of you don't resolve your differences?

Brandt: I don't know.

Administrator: Should we bring Christian in so that you two can work together to solve your conflict?

Brandt: Will you be here? (Obviously, he wanted outside support for solving his problem.)

Administrator: Yes, I will be here.

Brandt: OK.

(Christian, who meantime has been working on a plan in the RTC with the help of Nola Johnson, is brought to the administrator's office to learn to negotiate with Brandt on how to resolve their conflict. As the students are guided through the negotiation process, they begin to learn how to resolve their differences both in and out of school. It must always be remembered that you never allow students to begin negotiations until they are calm and settled sufficiently to work things out, and they are committed to resolving their problem.

Some schools insist that students work things out on their own. At first, I recommend that someone who is familiar with the strategies of the process assist the students so that they learn the necessary techniques. This will prepare them for future differences or conflicts by giving them the skills and confidence to work out problems on their own.

Christian has brought the plan he had been working on with the RTC teacher. Sometimes I have the students bring their plans with them, provided the plans have been completed.)

Administrator: Brandt, are you willing to work at solving the problem between you and Christian? (Testing the commitment of the student.)

Brandt: Yes, if he is. (Again, the student is trying to make what he does contingent upon what the other student does.)

Administrator: Brandt, who do you control?

Brandt: Me.

Administrator: Brandt, are you willing to work at solving the problem between you and Christian? (Repeating the above question to test for commitment.)

Brandt: Yes.

Administrator: Christian, how about you? Are you willing to work at solving the problem between you and Brandt?

Christian: I just want him to stay away from me. (Again, a contingent commitment, thus the question must be repeated.)

Administrator: Christian, are you willing to work at solving the problem between you and Brandt?

Christian: Yes.

Administrator: Brandt, what can you do to solve this problem?

Brandt: I can stop teasing Christian and making fun of him when we play basketball.

Administrator: Is that the only time you tease him?

Brandt: No, sometimes I tease him during class or when we are eating in the cafeteria.

Administrator: So, how can you help solve this problem?

Brandt: I guess I can stop teasing him wherever we are. (Whenever the student uses words like "I guess," that is a red flag, a sign of a weak commitment.)

Administrator: Brandt, are you really serious about this or not?

Brandt: Yes.

Administrator: Do you agree to stop teasing Christian and making fun of him?

Brandt: Yes.

Administrator: Christian, Brandt has agreed to stop teasing you. Will that help solve the problem?

Christian: He hit me, too.

Brandt: I didn't hit you.

Administrator: What are you two doing right now?

Christian: Arguing.

Administrator: Is arguing going to help solve the problem?

Brandt (looking at the floor): No, I guess not.

Christian: No.

Administrator: Christian, when you say that Brandt hit you, what do you mean?

Christian: He pushed me in the back.

Administrator: Brandt, are you willing to stop teasing and pushing Christian?

Brandt: Yes, if he'll stop pushing me.

Administrator: Brandt, who is it you control?

Brandt: Me.

Administrator: Brandt, are you willing to stop teasing and pushing Christian? (Remember to always keep the students focused on what they control and are willing to do, regardless of what others do.)

Brandt: Yes.

Administrator: Christian, if Brandt stops teasing and pushing you, will this help solve the problem?

Christian: Yes.

Administrator: Christian, what are you willing to do to help solve the problem between you and Brandt?

Christian: If he'll stop teasing and pushing me, I won't push or hit him.

Administrator: Can you control what Brandt does?

Christian: No.

Administrator: Who is it you control, and who am I talking with right now? (Again, when students try to avoid taking responsibility for their actions, you must focus them on the issue at hand until they are willing to commit to working on what *they* can do, regardless of what others do.)

Christian: Me.

Administrator: So, what are you willing to do to help solve the problem between you and Brandt?

Christian: I won't push or hit him.

Administrator: Are you really serious about this?

Christian: Yes.

Administrator: So, what will you do the next time someone teases or makes fun of you?

Christian: I'll walk away.

Administrator: Can you really do that?

Christian: Yes.

Administrator: If that doesn't work, and the student continues to bother you, what will you do then?

Christian: I'll tell the teacher.

Administrator: Brandt, what is your plan if Christian or someone else pushes or hits you?

Brandt: I'll tell the teacher.

Administrator: What do you think of Christian's idea of walking away?

Brandt: If they push me, I could walk away, but if they hit me, I don't think I could just walk away.

Administrator: Then what are you going to do if they hit you?

Brandt: I would probably try to hit them back.

Administrator: What happens when you hit someone at school, whatever the reason?

Brandt: You get sent to the RTC, and you could be suspended from school.

Administrator: Is that what you'd want?

Brandt: No.

Administrator: Does hitting someone back usually make things better or worse?

Brandt: Worse.

Administrator: So, what could you do if someone hit you?

Brandt: I could tell them I don't want to get suspended from school and walk away.

Administrator: Do you think that would work?

Brandt: I can try it.

Administrator: What if either of you were really angry, and you were having a hard time calming down, what could you do?

Christian and Brandt: I don't know.

Administrator: We have one student who loses his temper a lot. He solves that problem by going to the RTC and timing himself out until he calms down. What do you think of that idea?

Brandt: I like that. My friend, Nelson, does that now. He goes to the RTC every time he's ready to explode.

Administrator: What about you, Christian? Do you think you can do that when you get angry?

Christian: Yeah, I can try it.

Administrator: After you've calmed down in the RTC, what could you do?

Christian: I don't know.

Brandt: Go back to where we came from.

Administrator: Christian, would that work for you?

Christian: Yes.

Administrator: After you've calmed down, what could you do if you still had a problem with someone else?

Brandt: I don't know.

Administrator: What are we doing right now?

Christian: We're working our problems out with you.

Administrator: Is that something you could do if you have a problem in the future?

Brandt: Yeah.

Administrator: Christian, how about you?

Christian: Yes, I could do that.

(At this point, the administrator summarizes what has been agreed to by the two boys.)

Administrator: Let me see if I understand what both of

you have agreed to. Brandt, you are agreeing to stop teasing and pushing Christian, is that correct?

Brandt: Yes.

Administrator: Christian, you're agreeing to stop pushing and hitting Brandt, is that correct?

Christian: Yes.

Administrator: Both of you also agreed to walk away or tell a teacher if you have problems in the future. Is that right?

Christian and Brandt: Yes.

Administrator: You also agreed to time yourself out in the RTC when you get really angry, is that correct?

Brandt: Yes.

Administrator: Christian, how about you? (Always make sure you get responses to your questions.)

Christian: Yes, I agree.

Administrator: Are you willing to put your agreement in writing and sign it? (Again, testing their commitment.)

Christian: Yes, I am.

Brandt: Me, too.

Administrator: What do you think should happen to the person who breaks this agreement? (At this time, the administrator begins to fill out a conflict resolution form. See the sample form at the end of this chapter.)

Brandt: He has to report to the RTC.

Christian: And he could get suspended from school.

Administrator: To whom will you report any violation of this agreement?

Christian: To the teacher.

Brandt: To you, because you've helped us.

(The administrator completes the conflict resolution form, making sure to include everything to which the students have agreed. The students then sign the form, confirming their commitment to their agreement.

Brandt goes to the RTC to begin working on his plan with Ms. Johnson. She is given a copy of the agreement so that it can be used during the planning process. This agreement will also be included in the student's discipline record.

Christian stays with the administrator, who goes over the plan previously completed in the RTC. The administrator will work with Christian and review his plan, helping him to revise his plan where necessary, and making sure that all points are covered from the discussion with Brandt.)

Once their agreement is signed and their individual plans are completed and approved by the administrator, he can then discuss privately the consequences of each student's previous actions.

When consequences are discussed, the following points should be considered:

1. Did the student take responsibility for his actions?
2. Did the student willingly work to solve his problem?
3. How serious are the actions? (For example, teasing and pushing versus hitting or physical assault.)
4. The disciplinary history of each student.
5. District and school guidelines for specific student actions.

Throughout the questioning process, you will notice that regardless of how the students acted, the administrator kept the problem from escalating by never threatening, always asking questions in a calm, relaxed manner, and letting the students determine when they were ready to resolve the problem. He also had the students use the rules and expectations of the school as guidelines for evaluating how successful they were in controlling their own perceptions without disturbing others. This was evident each time the administrator asked "What's the rule?" and "What happens when you break the rule?"

Also, notice how the administrator continually respected the students' decisions and never criticized or threatened them or gave them advice. He always asked what the student wanted to do, and if what he was doing was working. He kept the students focused on the problem and never allowed them to digress into blaming others or trying to excuse what happened.

In following this process, the administrator should not be perceived as a disturbance or part of the students' problem, but rather as a caring person who is trying to help them. Brandt asked the administrator "Will you be there?" It was evident that he perceived the administrator as someone who was helping him work through the problem, and not as someone who was there to judge and punish him. When you are not trying to control students' actions, you are less likely to be perceived as a disturbance. Remember, disturbances are those things that get in the way of what we are trying to accomplish.

Often, you see the students struggle as they go through the questioning process, but that struggle is necessary if they are to learn to deal with their conflicts with any degree of skill and self-confidence. The administrator who makes all the decisions for the students never allows that struggle to take place, thus the students have little chance of developing that confidence on their own. They might also perceive the administrator as part of their problem, rather than as someone who teaches them how to find the solution. It is necessary to allow students adequate time to struggle through the process. It is that personal struggle, supported by a caring, patient person, that is critical to their developing self-confidence.

As students resolve conflicts, they develop the confidence needed to deal successfully with their own problems. This is why it is so important to introduce the negotiating process to students. They learn to use it in future difficulties and not to depend on someone else to mediate their problems. It is not uncommon to find students breaking up fights and arguments on their own several months after RTP has been introduced. When students can't solve their problems on their own, instead of fighting, they come to my office and ask for assistance.

During the questioning process, notice how the students changed their style of dealing with their conflict from the usual blaming and making excuses to focusing on resolving their problem. This is what happens when students learn this process. Also, without dealing with excuses, the problem solving time is reduced considerably. Even though it might seem to take a little more time at the beginning to help them deal with their conflict, the time is well spent.

What do you do with students who are unwilling to settle their differences? You simply ask them whether they will be able to stay away from each other until they can resolve their conflict. If they agree, you fill in their names on the conflict resolution form, where it states: "These students were unable to resolve their conflict. However, they agree to stay away from each other until they are able to solve their problems." Also, you fill in the consequences section, stating what happens when the agreement is violated.

If the students do not resolve their differences and are unwilling to stay away from each other, they return to the RTC. Once they develop an acceptable plan of action that will assure their conflict will not continue, they may return to class. When given this alternative, most students decide to find a way to resolve their differences or agree to stay away from each other. Remember, you never try to force students to resolve their disagreements. Only they can decide when they are ready. You never push on a living control system.

Instead of solving problems for students, RTP teaches them to solve their own problems. Through this process, students not only take responsibility for the problems, but also for the solutions. They are learning a process that will serve them throughout their lives. Isn't that what any discipline program should be about?

CONFLICT RESOLUTION THROUGH NEGOTIATION

These students have resolved their conflict and agree that the problem is resolved.

Students: _____

_____

These students were unable to resolve their conflict. However, they agree to stay away from each other until they are able to solve their problems.

Students: _____

_____

Agreement:

_____

_____

_____

_____

Consequences:

_____

_____

_____

_____

_____   _____
Administrator/RTC teacher   Date

_____   _____
Student   Student

_____   _____
Student   Student

_____   _____
Student   Student

Chapter 19
The Responsible Thinking Process, the Special Needs Child, and Special Education Mandates

LeEdna Custer-Knight
School Psychologist
Clarendon Elementary School
Osborn School District
Phoenix, Arizona

I am often asked, "What do you do when RTP isn't working?" Invariably, I then hear about a particular child who is spending most or all of the school day in the RTC or at home. In these instances, it is important to note that the process *is* working: the teacher is teaching, the other students have a nondisruptive learning environment, and the child is being allowed to choose to leave the classroom. However, most educators are disturbed to find a child frequently out of the classroom. What is the appropriate course of action? Perhaps, no action. Just as some children learn to walk or talk later than others, some children require more time to develop the skills of self-discipline (i.e., thinking and acting responsibly). But when it appears clear that the child is truly struggling to no avail, or he appears content to be removed from the educational process and socialization with peers, intervention is appropriate.

Federal legislation (IDEA and 504) requires all schools to have a referral process for identification and service of students with special needs. The misfortune is that, in many schools, this process is used primarily as a means of funneling students from regular education into the evaluation process and possible special education placement. The most important purpose this can serve is to attempt to discover for what the child is controlling and how the staff might help him to achieve his goals without infringing on the rights of others. An intervention team should work to discover modifications which will enable the child to successfully participate in his education. This might be as simple as giving the student time-out passes, allowing the choice of leaving the classroom, rather than disrupting, and then returning when ready. However, the team could find the task far more challenging. Hopefully, at least one member of the team has developed a relationship with the child and has asked what it is he really wants, what he perceives as a disturbance (as getting in the way of goal attainment), and how things might work out so that he could achieve his goals without interfering with the rights of others. Often, many attempts have already been made to have the child express what he wants and what is getting in the way, but to no avail. In many instances, the child's response is limited to the specific incident which has resulted in his current referral to the RTC. When probed further as to what the child perceives as the reason he is so often in the RTC, the response is "I don't know," "People tick me off," or "This school sucks!" Controlling is automatic, not conscious— the individual does not reflect on underlying causation.

How should you proceed when the child does not provide insight? You should attempt to create successful modifications. The keys to successful modifications are these:

1. *Look for patterns.* I cannot stress enough the importance of careful recordkeeping in the RTC. Our RTC teacher has prepared monthly calendars with highlighted RTC visits, absences, suspensions, etc. These visual aids are of great assistance in looking for patterns that might shed light on what a child wants, what are perceived disturbances, and how to negotiate so as to reduce errors to acceptable levels while not infringing on the rights of others. Looking at patterns can help detect times of day, classes, peers, and teachers that are consistently associated with RTC referrals and specific types of activities. Some students have trouble

with unstructured situations, such as changing classes, recess, and lunch. In such cases, we have had good results when the child moves to his next class five minutes before or after other students. Another useful strategy is supervised play in a designated area with one or two friends, rather than having the full reign of the playground. Once success is demonstrated, the area of play and/or the number of peers playing together can be increased.

2. *Be flexible.* Do not automatically assume your suggestions can't, won't, or shouldn't be attempted. Do not worry that other students will resent differences in how a student with special needs works things out. I have found that children understand and accept individual differences—often more readily than adults.

3. *Be creative.* One of our most successful modifications was for a child who had suffered a traumatic brain injury. He was extremely impulsive, explosive, and aggressive. It was suggested that when he started to feel angry, he could put his hands into his pockets. He agreed to try this, and it was amazingly effective. The time it took to put his hands in and then pull them out seemed to put enough distance between the impulse and the act to allow him to think and choose to stop.

4. *Be nonjudgmental.* Often, the outcomes of a child's choices do not reflect intended damage. Rather, the damage is an unintended consequence of pursuing a goal singlemindedly, i.e., Ted knocked down a peer when he pursued the ball; John hit a peer in a rage, later saying, "I really didn't mean to hurt him, I just wanted him to stop calling me names." Withholding judgment does not mean the child is not responsible for the outcome. It means not attributing outcomes to assumed character defects within the child.

5. *Negotiate.* Always keep in mind that the purpose of a modification is to assist the child in finding a means of resolving a conflict between his wants and the rights of others. You cannot solve the problem, and you cannot make him solve the problem. You will only create more

conflict if you attempt to impose rather than negotiate a modification, when imposing a "modification" becomes a euphemism for punishment.

6. *Work to create a quality relationship with the child and his parents.* This might seem elementary; however, often the most difficult child is the one who does not appear to be "connected" to anyone and who resists attempts to develop a relationship with others. Sometimes the child seems to have strong peer relationships (as in gangs) but resists developing relationships with adults. When your efforts are consistently rebuffed and a child is truly difficult, continuing to be invitational is at best a challenge. But it is a challenge worth taking. I have always found the time and difficulty of developing a relationship to be far less than dealing with the consequences of the alternative. Prisons are full of the unconnected and disenfranchised members of our society; their wreckage is what is left behind.

Developing a positive relationship with the parent or parents of a child experiencing difficulties in school can often be as difficult as with the child. Parents of children who are not experiencing success at school might feel the school blames them. Unfortunately, this *is* sometimes the case, implicitly or explicitly. I have known parents who have been told, "You need to ..." or "If you can't or won't or don't help your child study, how can you expect him to learn?" Often, well-intentioned suggestions result in parents who can't comply and who feel that the school judges them to be inadequate, and they withdraw or become hostile and defensive. Sometimes the parents' own difficulties make relationships difficult or even impossible. Cases where relationships are impossible are usually those where serious issues of abuse and neglect are present and the parent is truly unable to even minimally be a parent. Those require the intervention of child protection agencies and law enforcement officials.

Even when cases have been deemed hopeless, I have seen relationships with parents forged for the welfare of the child. Several years ago, I was feeling frustrated and hopeless when trying to deal with the ravages of drug addiction, violence, and poverty present in many of the families whose children we were charged to educate. I knew something had to change. I knew I couldn't change them. I chose to change myself. I chose and continue to choose to believe that within all parents is a seed of love for their child. That seed might be small, dry, and brittle, but it is there. I can choose to nourish or deny it. I speak about what I find of beauty, of wonderment, of joy, and of humor in the life they have created. I do not lie, gush, or placate. To do this effectively requires that I know their child. Maybe I have seen the impish grin right before the outburst; or the way, when he steals the ball from others, he runs gracefully, easily outdistancing them; or the intelligence in her eyes when she chooses the perfect insult guaranteed to send the recipient into a rage of tears. Often, it is a testament to their gifts that difficult children can create such disturbances for others.

7. *Be observant.* By careful observation, without judgment, you can find the greatest strengths a child possesses. Those could be the qualities on which to build your own more positive view of the child. Parents who know that you see great value in their children are more willing to work with you rather than oppose you.

8. *Use a questioning process with parents, instead of telling and demanding.* Questioning acknowledges you are there to serve, not dictate. "What is it that you want for John?" "Do you think ... might work?" "Do you have suggestions?" "What do you find effective at home?" Even when a parent is angry, demanding, and unreasonable, questioning can help, starting with "What is it that you want for John?" and moving to "Do you think taking responsibility for ... is going to help him be successful?" When parents are demanding something inappropriate, questions can help them reference higher-level goals for their children which conflict with what they currently want ("I want John to get a good education and have an easier life than I do." "Do you think that taking responsibility for his work is going to help

him get that?") I have found that success in working with difficult parents comes from speaking to their love, even when I cannot see it, and from being ever-mindful that my job is one of service.

How do intervention teams and modifications relate to special education? First, as stated earlier, the teams can serve the legally required purpose of referral and identification of children with possible handicapping conditions. The documentation of interventions can demonstrate that significant alternatives have been attempted prior to special education; this is a very important component in determining what is the least restrictive environment necessary to educate the child. In terms of a child already served in special education, the modifications become a part of his Individual Education Plan. The entire responsible thinking process appears aligned not only with the intent but also with the requirements of federal legislation.

Chapter 20
RTP and the Pre-School and Primary Special Education Classrooms

Carmen Duron
Special Education Pre-School Teacher
Solano Elementary School
Osborn School District
Phoenix, Arizona

and

Erin Powell
Special Education Primary School Teacher
Squaw Peak Elementary School
Creighton Elementary School District
Phoenix, Arizona

The authors of this chapter have had great success with RTP techniques under extraordinarily difficult conditions. I am tremendously impressed by their pioneering work in adapting the RTP questioning technique with these young-sters. I remember back to the first time Carmen invited me to her class to observe and offer suggestions as to how she could use RTP. I had no previous experience with children with disabilities. Carmen was working with four children playing with clay. I was behind her, watching. At one point, Jamie, a three-year-old with Down's Syndrome, began to choke another student. I whispered to Carmen, "Just ask him, 'What are you doing?'" Carmen did so, and Jamie turned, looked at Carmen, and slowly withdrew his hands from his classmate's throat. Then Jamie began to gently stroke the back of the student's head, as if to say, "I'm sorry."

Carmen looked in disbelief and then said, "Wow! He under-stands more than I gave him credit for." From then on, Car-men and I worked closely together. Now I have the chance to say "Wow!" about how far she and Erin have taken RTP, and about what they have learned and accomplished since that modest beginning.

—*Ed Ford*

The children discussed in this chapter are from two self-contained special education classrooms. One of the class-rooms serves three- to four-year-old children. Their dis-abilities include moderate cognitive delays, expressive and receptive language delays, physical impairments, and mod-erate to severe behavioral disorders. The other classroom serves five- to nine-year-old children. Their disabilities in-clude mild to severe mental retardation, autism, emotion-al impairments, visual impairments, other physical impair-ments, and combinations of these disabilities.

Both classrooms are language- and sensory-based. We believe that the teacher must nurture the child's intent to interact with his world and create an understanding of it. Providing an environment conducive for exploration and ample opportunities for children to make decisions cannot be complete without the children learning about how to deal with the consequences of their actions. A child's natu-ral desire to interact with the world and make his own choices often brings him into conflict with both other chil-dren and adults.

How does the child learn that some of what he does will interfere with other people's rights? This is the heart of the matter. Some would say it is the responsibility of parents and schools to make the rules and enforce them. It is their responsibility to tell the child what is "right" and what is "wrong." Yet, time and again, we meet children who do not appear to "know the rules" of appropriate social behavior, despite repeated reprimands and shaming by parents, schools, and others. How can we educate a child within the classroom if he hasn't learned to respect the rights of others? If he hasn't learned to obey the rules of wherever he is, his successes in life very likely will be limited.

Thus, we believe that children must learn to become aware of others around them, especially when their own goals are in conflict with what others are trying to accomplish. They must be taught to be aware of the consequences of their actions as they try to control their perceptions, especially when others have what they want or are in the way of what they are trying to accomplish. The child must be able to think about the consequences of his actions if he is to get along, whether in the classroom, at home, or in the larger community in which he lives.

When we first heard Ed speak about RTP, we were both skeptical. Could some of these children with disabilities really understand right from wrong? As we began to look at the research, we found that cognitive understanding of right and wrong could be seen as early as 18 months. This, however, was in the normally developing child. Our youngest child was three years old, but all of them had disabilities. In the current literature, as well as at conferences and in university classes, we never found an effective way for teaching our specific children the necessary skills for following rules and respecting others.

If the goal is to help the child learn to respect the rights of others, then parents and teachers must find a way to teach children to think about how they might control their perceptions while not interfering with other children's rights to do the same thing. The child must learn to think about the *effects* of his actions on others if he is to get along, whether in the classroom, at home, or in the larger community. RTP provides a method that lays the foundation for the child to learn "why" certain ways of controlling perceptions are appropriate and "why" others are not. Interestingly, the method never uses the word "why" in any of its questions. Here is an example to illustrate this. Matthew wanted a toy, and he punched Frank, who had the toy. Frank cried, while Matthew looked on. The teacher entered the scene, and in a calm, curious voice, she asked Matthew,

"What are you doing?" Frank answered, "He kicked me!" Another teacher took Frank aside.

Teacher (to Matthew): What are you doing?

Matthew: I wanted the toy. He wouldn't give it to me.

Teacher: What did you do to Frank?

Matthew: I wanted the toy.

Teacher: Is it OK to kick Frank?

Matthew (speaking slowly): No.

Teacher: What happens when you kick him?

Matthew: I can't play with the toy.

Teacher: Is that what you want?

Matthew: No.

Teacher: What do you want?

Matthew: I want to play with the toy.

Teacher (continuing to probe): Is punching Frank going to allow you to play with the toy?

Matthew: No.

Teacher: Who was playing with the toy?

Matthew: Frank.

Teacher: What could you play with while Frank's playing with the toy?

Matthew: The other one.

Teacher: Can you play with the other toy until it's your turn?

Matthew: Yes.

In this example, the teacher helped Matthew make a simple plan, according to his ability to learn how to control his perception without creating any disruptive consequences.

The next example shows how Anthony, a child with severe behavioral problems, created a plan. Anthony could not be near another child without punching, spitting, pulling hair, and biting. He showed a great deal of anger toward adults. When he became angry, he would bite and kick teachers. Anthony generally stayed on the fringes of the classroom. He rarely played or interacted with peers. Teachers' invitations to play or interact were ignored, and if they touched him as a way of including him into the activity, Anthony would scream, moving farther away. In this example, Anthony and the teacher were in the classroom's manipulative area. This is the area that contains equipment such as pegs, beads, and puzzles for developing fine motor skills involving the manipulation of objects with fingers. Anthony wanted a red bead that another child was holding. He started to take the bead from the child.

Teacher: What are you doing?

Anthony: Taking red bead.

Teacher: Is that OK?

Anthony (on the verge of a tantrum): Me take red bead.

Teacher: Is that OK to take away the bead?

Anthony: Me want red bead.

Teacher: What happens when you take things from others?

Anthony: I don't know.

Teacher: What would happen if someone took a bead from you?

Anthony: I don't know.

Teacher: Would you like for me to take what you're playing with?

Anthony: No ... me want bead.

Teacher: Is it OK to take away the bead from Preston?

Anthony: No.

Teacher: Could you play with this yellow bead while Preston plays with the red bead?

Anthony: Yes.

Teacher: Could you ask Preston if you could have the red bead when he is done playing with it?

Anthony: Yes.

Teacher: So what are you going to ask Preston?

Anthony: Can I have bead when you done?

Teacher: So when do you get the bead?

Anthony: When he done.

Anthony went on to play with another bead. He experienced success. He took the teacher's advice, and the other child gave the bead to him. Anthony's willingness to deal with the teacher without a tantrum was quite remarkable, given the fact that he normally would have behaved in a very angry and emotionally distraught way. The one-on-one quality time with the teacher (see Chapter 6) made it easier for the teacher to interact with Anthony. The development of his plan enabled him to think through what he wanted and how to get it appropriately.

To gauge our success in providing quality time for every child, we use a chart with the names of the children on the left and dates going across the top. For each date, there is a box next to the child's column. When a teacher spends at least two to three minutes of continuous one-on-one time alone with a child, she marks the time on the chart and initials it. The chart shows, at a glance, the amount of quality time being spent with each child. We have discovered that as quality time increases, defiant behavior decreases.

Another example: Three children were playing with the class bunny. They were very interested in holding the bunny's leash, which was around his neck. One of the teachers heard the children yelling and saw that Sam and Ellen were tugging at the leash in opposite directions.

Teacher: What are you doing?

Ellen: He won't give me the leash!

Sam: It's my turn to hold the leash!

Teacher: What is the rule?

Ellen: We supposed to take turns. It's my turn.

Teacher: Is pulling on the leash going to hurt the bunny?

Sam: I don't know.

Teacher: If you had a rope around your neck, and I pulled it, would it hurt? (This technique of connecting a personal experience that the child would understand to an unintended consequence of what the child is doing helps the child make the connection between his own actions and what others might be experiencing.)

Ellen: Yes.

Teacher: Is it OK to hurt the bunny?

Sam: No.

Teacher: What happens when you don't follow the rules?

Sam: You put bunny in his cage.

Teacher: Is that what you want?

Sam and Ellen: No!

Teacher: What do you want?

Sam: We want to play with bunny.

Teacher: Is fighting over the bunny going to get you what you want?

Ellen: No.

Teacher: What can you do to get what you want?

Sam: I can go first, then you can look at your watch when it's Ellen's turn. (When a child comes up with a plan, whether it has been used before or not, this is an indication of the growing maturity of the child.)

Teacher: Ellen, what do you think about what Sam said?

Ellen: OK. But you'll watch the time.

Teacher: That's a deal!

The teacher gently but firmly assisted the children in remembering the rule by asking about it. At the same time, she communicated to them that *they* were making the decisions. Ultimately, they had to think about the choice of whether they were to play with the bunny or not. Always, the role of the teacher is one of a facilitator.

Before RTP, we attempted a variety of approaches for handling disruptions. We tried a myriad of techniques, including "time out," token systems, and "if-then" reasoning. None of these techniques had a long-lasting impact. Usually, the children resumed their disruptions immediately after or at some later point. In addition, it appeared as if the children perceived the teacher as "the bad guy"; they would direct their anger toward the teacher. The more we used RTP, the more students and teachers developed a mutually caring, nurturing, and loving relationship. We began to see that through the questioning process, we were showing these youngsters respect through our acceptance of their answers as *their* answers. Under the old method of telling and yelling, they would sense that we were trying to control them. The situation invariably got worse. By our using a calm, respectful, and curious approach, the students became less threatened, tended to calm down, and were more willing to interact with us. Mutual respect was created, and, at the same time, goals were achieved.

Another problem with the techniques we had been using was that the children did not connect their behavior with the intended or unintended consequences of their actions. They became more manipulative and did not think about the consequences of their actions. Invariably, the disruptions continued: A teacher observed Jacob punching Timmy in the arm, unaware that Timmy had taken Jacob's book. The teacher would have said to Jacob, "No, you may not hit, go to time out." Jacob might have felt frustrated. He did not have the verbal skills to express himself. He might have lost faith in his teacher. No thinking was involved on his part. And most importantly, mutual respect was absent. The application of RTP methods created quite different results.

Teacher to Timmy and Jacob: What are you two doing?

Jacob: He took the book I was reading.

Teacher: What did you do?

Jacob: I punched him.

Teacher: Is it OK to punch?

Jacob: No.

Teacher: What happens when you hit?

Jacob: I have to leave the group.

Teacher: Will you be able to look at books if you hit someone?

Jacob: No.

Teacher: What could you do the next time someone takes away the book you are reading?

Jacob: I don't know.

Teacher: Could you get another book?

Jacob: Yes.

Teacher: Now, what are you going to do the next time someone takes your book? (Since the plan was suggested by the teacher, it was best to ask a second time, to make sure the plan was understood and was part of what the student intended to do in the future.)

Jacob: I'll get another book.

In this example, the teacher did a number of things. First, she *listened* to Jacob. She did not jump to conclusions. Second, she asked Jacob questions that helped him think. She also assisted him in making a plan for handling similar situations in the future. The teacher did not alienate Jacob but rather maintained mutual respect. The teacher also asked Timmy similar questions:

Teacher: What are you doing?

Timmy: He punched me.

Teacher: What were you doing?

Timmy: I want to read this book.

Teacher: What did you do to get that book?

Timmy: I took it.

Teacher: Is that OK?

Timmy: No.

Teacher: What are the rules?

Timmy: We're not supposed to grab. We're supposed to ask.

Teacher: What happens when you break the rules?

Timmy: I can't look at the book.

Teacher: Is that what you want?

Timmy: No.

Teacher: Is taking away the book going to allow you to be in the group and look at the book?

Timmy: No.

Teacher: Next time you want a book that someone is looking at, what will you do?

Timmy: I will tell him, "I want the book next."

Teacher: If the child says, "No," what else could you do?

Timmy: Go to the teacher.

Teacher: Is there anything else you could do?

Timmy: I guess I could get another book. (Notice that the teacher did not praise the child for coming up with a correct answer. The real reward for the child was the building of his own self-confidence, something he created within himself.)

Here, the teacher helped the child think about what he could do next time. He was not shamed or made to feel embarrassed. It is unfortunate that adults use rewards and punishments to control children's behavior. "Doing something" to a child takes away his dignity by not respecting his own ability to resolve his problems. What's worse, the teacher then *becomes* the problem. Instead, violating others' rights should be perceived by the child as *his* problem.

Through its questioning format, RTP reveals what is happening *within* the child—what he is experiencing. RTP is not concerned with what the teacher thought she saw the child do, or what she heard, or what other children thought or heard about what the child did or did not do. Each individual has his own way of thinking. RTP respects the child's viewpoint, while at the same time helping each child to respect others and follow the rules. Interestingly, children eventually learn the purpose of rules: to serve as useful guides to help them live in harmony with others. We know this is happening when we see them treat other children with respect.

Frankie ran over to a teacher, complaining that John was taking the blocks he was using for building. Frankie was quite upset, and the teacher calmly walked over to the block area:

Teacher (to John): What are you doing?

John: They are my blocks.

Teacher: I saw you take blocks from other children. Is that OK?

John: Yes.

Teacher: What are the rules for building with blocks?

John: Blocks stay on the floor, and I have to share the blocks.

Teacher: What are you doing?

John: I don't want to give Frankie my blocks.

Teacher: Is that OK?

John: No.

Teacher: What happens when you don't share?

John: I can't play.

Teacher: Is that what you want?

John: No.

Teacher: What do you want, now?

John: To build with the blocks.

Teacher: If you do not give blocks to Frankie, will you be allowed to play?

John: No.

Teacher: What do you have to do if you want to play with the blocks?

John: Give Frankie some of my blocks.

Teacher: How will that help?

John: I'll get along with Frankie.

It is very important that the teacher never indicate disapproval. Shaming is not a part of RTP.

As we mentioned earlier, RTP allows for mutual respect to build between the students and teachers. Ultimately, we've watched the children slowly develop the same respect for each other. The following example demonstrates how the process respects the child. Robert, who has a low frustration tolerance, threw a pegboard across the room.

Teacher (in a calm voice): What are you doing?

Robert (angry): Nothing!

Teacher: Did you throw the pegboard across the room?

Robert (crying): My fingers are too big. I can't fit the little pegs into the holes!

Teacher (touching Robert and speaking to him in a caring voice): Is that OK to throw the pegboard across the room?

Robert: No.

Teacher: Could other children get hurt when you throw the pegboard?

Robert: Yes.

Teacher: What do you want now?

Robert: I want to get the little pegs into the holes!

Teacher: Is throwing the pegboard going to get the little pegs into the holes?

Robert: No.

Teacher: Do you want to learn how to put the little pegs into the holes?

Robert: Yes.

Teacher: Who could help you?

Robert (pausing and looking around): A teacher.

Teacher: The next time you need help, who will you ask to help you?

Robert (smiling): A teacher.

In using the RTP questions, the teacher was able to help Robert explore what was on his mind. She respected Robert by being patient and helping him to work through his frustration by using the questioning process. In the end, Robert had a plan for what he could do the next time.

RTP is especially powerful for children who perceive themselves as powerless, as having no control over their lives. It provides teachers with a framework from which they can help children express what is on their minds. Then, children can experience the power within them to make choices that will get them what they want.

During clean-up time, Freddie was climbing up and down a triangle. A teacher approached him.

Teacher: Freddie, what are you doing?

Freddie (before the teacher could ask "Is that OK?"): Climbing the triangle, and it's not OK.

With RTP, children increasingly think for themselves. No other process that we know fosters this. In the above case, the teacher did not need to pose any more questions. Freddie participated in clean-up and then washed for snack time.

One hectic morning, four children were wrestling on the other side of the classroom. It so happened that two of our four teachers were absent. At that moment, the two remaining teachers were occupied on the other side of the room. One of them called out, "What are you doing?" The children who were wrestling stopped, looked over at the teacher, and one by one went to another area of the room and became engaged in other activities.

In time, children understand the process quite well—so well that they begin cueing each other. For instance, a teacher was working with Chris. Amelia, who was nearby, began tossing pieces of playdough.

Teacher: What are you doing?

Chris (looking at Amelia, who was staring speechless at the teacher): Throwing the playdough.

Amelia: Throw playdough.

We are frequently asked by parents, directly or indirectly, how their child is getting along with other children. Is he following the rules and respecting teachers? RTP is a great resource for communicating with parents. We discuss each of the RTP questions and their child's responses to them.

Initially, in their struggle to deal with the rules, some children become annoyed and angered by the questions. But as they experience the questions and thus learn that there is consistency, fairness, and a calmness, we have found that the children become more and more open to participating. Over time, with rare exceptions, our children learn that each one of them is responsible for his own behavior. When children antagonize an adult with the consequences of their actions, this usually results in criticism or punishment. RTP's direct approach eliminates the crying and tantrums. With RTP, when children exhibit tantrums (hitting, screaming, or crying), an adult waits for the child to calm down before asking the RTP questions. Once the child is ready to talk, RTP can be used systematically and effectively.

Some people are skeptical about using RTP questions for children with special needs. After all, many of them have language and cognitive delays. RTP requires children to answer what for them are complex questions that challenge them to think. RTP provides a format for *learning how* to answer questions; the questions relate to what the child is experiencing, thus the questions are meaningful to him. However, there are some children who do need extra teacher support to follow the questioning process. Augmentative devices, pictures, modeling, hand-over-hand assistance, and modifying the questions are important tools, especially for children with severe language and cognitive disabilities. Overlays can be custom-made to fit a variety of situations. The simplest overlay is the "Yes/No." Overlays can become more complicated by adding classroom rules and vocabulary related to RTP.

Shantel, a non-verbal child with autism, uses a 36-grid overlay on a communication device to answer the RTP questions. (See diagram below.) The first row allows Shantel to answer the question "What are you doing?" This row has pictures and phrases that depict her most common disruptions. The second row allows Shantel to answer the question "What are the rules?" The third row allows Shantel to answer the question "What happens when you break the rules?" The fourth row allows Shantel to answer the question "What do you want to happen now?" The fifth row allows Shantel to answer the question "What do you need to get what you want?" Finally, the sixth row allows Shantel

to choose to work or not to work. We can also ask other important questions related to a disruption, phrasing them as questions with Yes/No answers. This overlay is a fairly complicated example; with it, Shantel can participate successfully in the responsible thinking process.

Jason, a nonverbal child with severe cognitive and physical impairments, hit a classmate to get her attention. Although Jason was beginning to follow one-step directions related to the daily routine, he did not understand the questioning process. He needed a two-grid overlay with Yes/No on it to help him through the questioning process.

Teacher (showing augmentative device with Yes/No overlay to Jason): What are you doing?

Jason: (No response.)

Teacher (with a hitting motion as a visual cue): Were you hitting Kim?

Jason: (Points to "No" on overlay.)

Teacher (pointing to "Yes" on overlay): Yes, you hit Kim.

Jason: (Points to "Yes" on overlay.)

Teacher: What are the rules?

Jason: (Points to rule chart displayed on wall at child's eye level. The chart is a poster with words and pictures of classroom rules.)

Teacher (pointing to picture on rule chart of child holding his hands on his lap): We keep our hands to ourselves.

Jason: (Points to picture on rule chart.)

Teacher: What happens when you break the rules?

Jason: (No response.)

Teacher: Do you go to the RTC?

Jason: (Points to "Yes" on overlay.)

Teacher: Is that what you want to happen?

Jason: (Points to "Yes" on overlay.)

Teacher (pointing to door leading to RTC): Do you want to go visit the RTC room? (Pointing to "No" on overlay.) No, you want to be with the group.

Jason: (Also points to "No" on overlay.)

Teacher: What do you need to do to stay in the group?

Jason: (No response.)

Teacher (cueing for an alternative behavior): Do you want to wave at Kim?
Jason: (Waves at Kim.)
Teacher: What happens if you hit Kim again?
Jason: (No response.)
Teacher: Do you go to the RTC?
Jason: (Points to "Yes" on overlay.)
Teacher: OK, you're on caution.

The teacher then sends Jason to the caution chart to change the color of his name card from green to yellow. The caution chart is a poster on which each child has a name card (one side green, the other side yellow). The cards provide a reminder that they have been acting responsibly (green) or that they are on caution (yellow), so that the next disruption will result in visiting the RTC.

It is important to provide children with significant developmental delays many opportunities to follow through with their plans. For instance, Jason's plan was to wave to Kim to get her attention. The next time Jason hit Kim, the teacher would ask, while modeling the waving, "Are you following the plan?" Jason would then wave. Thus, he would get practice in following his plan. If he did not follow the plan and chose to hit Kim, the teacher would go through the questioning process again, and he would then visit the RTC.

Angela is a five-year-old with mild cognitive delays and severe language impairments. She expresses her wants by using one-word sentences. Angela answers questions with yes or no answers appropriately, but she has great difficulty answering "who," "what," "when," and "where" questions. Her goal was to answer the RTP questions using one word. The RTP method gave her the opportunity to learn how to respond to "who," "what," "when," and "where" questions within the context of the meaningful experiences that RTP provides. When the child breaks a rule, she becomes aware of her actions and works with her teacher to resolve the problem. Angela constantly grabbed objects that belonged to children and teachers. The art supplies were on a table, out of reach of all of the children. The teacher asked the children to sit at the art table and keep their hands on their laps. Angela reached over to grab the glue.

Teacher: What are you doing?
Angela: (No response.)
Teacher: Are you touching the glue?
Angela: Yes.
Teacher (modeling the answer): Tell me: "Touching."
Angela: Touching.
Teacher: What are you doing?
Angela: Touching.
Teacher: What is the rule?
Angela: (No response.)
Teacher: Is it to keep our hands to ourselves?
Angela: Yes.
Teacher: Tell me: "Hands."
Angela: Hands.
Teacher: What is the rule?
Angela (putting her hands on her lap): Hands, hands.
Teacher: What happens when you break the rules?
Angela: (No response.)
Teacher: Do you go to the RTC?
Angela: Yes.
Teacher: Tell me: "RTC."
Angela: RTC.
Teacher: What happens when you break the rules?
Angela: RTC.
Teacher: Is this what you want to happen?
Angela: No.
Teacher: What do you need to do to stay with the group?
Angela: (Pats her hands in her lap.)
Teacher: What happens when you disrupt again?
Angela: (No response.)
Teacher: Tell me: "RTC."
Angela: RTC.
Teacher: What happens when you disrupt again?
Angela: RTC.

Teacher: OK, you are on caution.

Angela: (Changes her name card on the caution chart to yellow.)

Jason and Angela initially needed teacher support, visual cues, and augmentative devices to answer the RTP questions. By the end of the school year, Angela was answering "what" questions appropriately and independently, using three- and four-word sentences. Jason was verbally answering questions with yes or no answers appropriately. Not only were they answering the questions appropriately, but Jason and Angela also displayed a greater respect for other students' rights as they followed their plans.

Classroom staff and eight-year-old Lee's mother were skeptical about her ability to understand and follow RTP. Lee is a very low-functioning nonverbal child with autism. On one occasion, Lee's mother was volunteering in the classroom. She observed the teacher employing RTP with Lee for the first time. The children were going through a simple obstacle course; Lee did not want to participate. She preferred to be left alone at all times. The teacher told her it was time to go through the obstacle course.

Teacher: What are you doing?

Lee: (Looks past the teacher, a common response for her.)

Teacher: Are you playing?

Lee: (Points to "No" on overlay.)

Teacher: What is the rule?

Lee: (Looks past the teacher.)

Teacher: Is it to follow directions?

Lee: (Points to "Yes" on overlay.)

Teacher: What happens when you break the rules?

Lee: (Looks past the teacher.)

Teacher: Do you go to the RTC?

Lee: (Points to "Yes" on overlay.)

Teacher: Is this what you want to happen?

Lee: (Points to "No" on overlay.)

Teacher: What do you need to do to stay with the group?

Lee: (Looks past the teacher.)

Teacher: Do you need to play?

Lee: (Points to "Yes" on overlay.)

Teacher: What happens when you disrupt again?

Lee: (Looks past the teacher.)

Teacher: Do you go to the RTC?

Lee: (Points to "Yes" on the overlay.)

Without another word from the teacher, Lee completed the obstacle course. Her mother and the classroom staff were shocked.

There will be times when a child refuses to respond to RTP. One approach is to calmly ask him to leave the group and sit in a quiet area in the classroom until he is ready to talk. Phillip was one of those children. He would not participate in RTP. He was asked to leave the group. Phillip left angrily. Ten minutes later, he returned, ready to speak. Phillip was "in control." He decided when he was ready. Another approach is to ask a child to leave the group and go to the RTC until he is ready to work.

Nine-year-old Amy, a child with multiple handicaps, learned RTP in a short time. Her DynaVox (an augmentative device) was programmed with RTP vocabulary. Amy insisted on accomplishing tasks in her own time. She could wait a long time when following simple directions or completing simple tasks. Many times, Amy refused to perform a task even when it was made desirable. Amy needed to push her wheelchair to the classroom next door. (She loved this class.)

Teacher: What are you doing?

Amy: (Turns head away from the teacher.)

Teacher: You need to go into your RTP page on your DynaVox.

Amy: (Takes teacher's hand and pushes the RTP button on her DynaVox.)

Teacher: What are you doing?

Amy: (Turns head away again.)

Teacher: Are you going to work with me? Remember, if you choose not to work with me, you choose to go to the RTC.

Amy: (Pushes the button for "I don't want to work now.")
Teacher: You've chosen to go to the RTC.

(Amy was taken to the RTC to make a plan for following directions. When the plan was completed and negotiated, she returned to the classroom.)

Teacher: Amy, push yourself to the classroom next door.

(Amy immediately pushed herself next door.)

If a child chooses not to work, he is given time in the RTC or away from the group, in the classroom, until he is ready to work. A teacher must judge when it is appropriate for the child to go either to the RTC or to an area in the classroom to develop a written or verbal plan. How a teacher makes this decision depends on how the RTC staff cooperate with the child and his teachers. Other considerations are the child's age and where the child best develops plans. (Never do Carmen's three- and four-year-olds go to the school RTC. They stay in the classroom. Erin's five- to eight-year-olds occasionally choose the RTC, and Erin works in close cooperation with the RTC staff.) An example of the latter case is when a child, regardless of being in another part of the classroom because he was disrupting in the group, might find ways to continue disrupting. Developing a plan in the classroom would not be appropriate, because the child is not willing to follow rules. In that case, it would be advisable to send the child to the RTC to develop a plan. If a child wants to be an active participant in class activities, he will be willing to develop a plan in the classroom.

A child's developmental age is important when determining if the child goes to a location within the classroom or visits the RTC. A child functioning at an infant level could find the RTC overwhelming and experience anxiety. Clearly, that child would be unable to develop a plan. If that child remained in the classroom, he could focus on the plan. Teachers must be flexible when determining the best location for making the plan.

When children with special needs visit the RTC, it is important to educate the RTC staff about each child's capabilities. For example, Amy, mentioned above, needed assistance in using her DynaVox augmentative device. Specifically, she had difficulty stabilizing her arm to push the buttons on her DynaVox. The special education teacher taught the RTC staff how to mobilize her arm so she could communicate with them. Frequent communication between the RTC staff and classroom staff must occur in order for there to be optimum success.

Many teachers, parents, and administrators think that children with special needs, pre-school to elementary, do not have the capability to respond to or understand RTP. It is our experience that when teachers make a conscious effort to help children participate in RTP, these children will rise to the occasion. They can learn to control their perceptions while, at the same time, respecting the rights of their peers, resulting in more time for learning, exploring, and playing.

Chapter 21
Challenges with Special Ed Students

Mark Hamel
Behavior Intervention Specialist
Amarillo Independent School District
Amarillo, Texas

It has been my experience over the past three years that if any method, technique, or process is going to be "used" or implemented with students in special education, the responsible thinking process should certainly lead the list. For 12 years prior to meeting and working with Ed Ford, I tried many behavior modification techniques, reinforcement methods, etc. All of the techniques and theories that I was taught and trained in at the college level only left me frustrated and feeling incompetent when working with special needs children. Basically, I was taught how to control students, while we all know that that is impossible and has a high failure rate.

As a Behavior Intervention Specialist with the Amarillo Independent School District, I work almost exclusively with students in special education, including children diagnosed with emotional disturbance, conduct disorder, oppositional defiant disorder, attention deficit disorder, attention deficit hyperactivity disorder, learning disability, mental retardation, fetal alcohol syndrome, autism, bipolar disorder, and other labels that psychologists use.

After becoming familiar with RTP and PCT and learning from Ed and others associated with the process, I felt compelled and confident enough to implement RTP with some of the students and teachers I work with on a regular basis. Even though I had read Ed's books and watched him in action, I still needed to go back to Amarillo and struggle with this process and what I had learned on my own. I quickly learned that a person doesn't become an expert on RTP and PCT simply by reading (and re-reading) books. As a teacher, specialist, or administrator, one must "get in the trenches" daily, as Ed terms it, and learn from experiences with each individual student. After three years in those trenches, I have learned a great deal—but there is still much to learn. Each day, students teach me a little more about human behavior and the perceptions we all carry around with us.

What follows is a short history of my three-year experience working with students daily, as well as working and teaching the teachers how to implement RTP. It is important to be trained by a certified trainer. School staff members should feel confident in the trainer's ability to teach the proper methods and techniques involved in working with living control systems.

Prior to bringing RTP into the Amarillo schools, I thought that it would be important for me to find a first-year teacher who would be willing and open to this "new" process. Although a first-year teacher was not essential, I felt that my chances and the teacher's chances would be greatly enhanced if someone right out of school would give this process an opportunity in the classroom.

It just so happened that I found such a teacher who was willing and eager to learn. Tammy Mason, a first-year teacher at one of our elementary schools, was enthusiastic about RTP. She read and re-read all of the materials I could provide her about RTP and PCT. Her ability to work with students, while maintaining mutual respect, is truly remarkable. She is truly dedicated to her students and strives daily to teach them to think for themselves and to become responsible, respectful students. But most of all, the students she has worked with since 1995 respect her and love to be in her classroom. She has no equal when teaching students to think and solve problems. Tammy is also known for passionately defending RTP, which shows how dedicated she is to this process and its potential. She is a very dedicated teacher, and I'm glad I chose her to be the first RTP teacher in Amarillo.

Paula Bowers, Tammy's assistant in the classroom, is also enthusiastic and willing to learn. Tammy has taught her well, and they both work very well together as a team. Paula uses the process well, and students treat her with respect, as they do Tammy.

Tammy's classroom is a self-contained classroom known as a BAC (behavior adjustment class) unit. In her classroom are about eight individual cubicles and a padded time-out booth with an observation window. In Tammy's unit are third, fourth, and fifth grade students, mostly male, with diagnoses of the kinds mentioned above. The unit is housed within the elementary school and usually has six to eight students.

Tammy was introduced to and trained in RTP starting in mid-October of 1995. This follow-up training continues today on a weekly basis. Back in 1995, we started by looking at some of her data prior to implementing RTP. She kept data on the number of physical restraints and the number of time-outs. Physical restraints were defined as actually having to hold a student in an approved restraining hold until the student regained control of his behavior, whether the student was standing or taken to the ground during the restraint. Time-out was defined as escorting a student to the time-out booth when the student became disruptive to the class, teacher, or learning environment.

From August 15 to October 15, 1995, Tammy had recorded 40 physical restraints and 40 time-outs. After learning RTP and implementing the process, the number of time-outs and physical restraints decreased dramatically. From October 16, 1995 to May 30, 1996 (the remainder of the school year), only seven time-outs and seven physical restraints had to be imposed on the students in her unit. Tammy and Paula became much more relaxed than before—better able to teach, and better able to do more activities with their students.

The following are examples of students who have been

in Tammy's class, and how they have become more successful with RTP. There have been many success stories since beginning RTP. Other teachers in the school became very interested; they too wanted to learn the techniques. Several BAC-unit students are now being "mainstreamed" into resource classes and regular education classes. Some of the reports have indicated that the students in the BAC unit are many times "better behaved" than mainstream students. RTP has given the students control of their world, and they now display self-confidence and control in stressful situations.

With a reduction in behavior problems over a two- to three-year period, academic achievement has been steadily rising. The grades of the BAC-unit students have increased an average of 10 points in each subject, and all of the objectives of their Individual Education Plans have been met. None of the other 12 BAC units in Amarillo can compare to Tammy's unit in the above-mentioned areas.

One fifth grade student, Parker, was very withdrawn and at times verbally aggressive prior to implementing RTP. Numerous restraints were used before Tammy became Parker's teacher. Since then, Parker has made improvements on the Brigance test from first grade levels in word recognition, oral reading, reading comprehension, spelling, and math to third grade levels in just one school year. During his third year in the BAC unit with RTP, he had zero physical restraints and very few time-outs.

Hollyann, another fifth grader, focused much of her time on trying to get others' attention inappropriately. Most of the time she was functioning on a third grade level; eventually she met her grade level requirements within the school year. She learned how to receive attention through her plan writing in more appropriate ways and was eventually released from the BAC unit to attend regular classes on a full-time basis.

Brent, a third grader, was very physically aggressive and had injured staff on occasion. He didn't care whom he hurt or how he hurt them. He displayed a lot of self-abusive behaviors, such as biting, scratching and hitting himself. He did not know how to control his anger and really had no desire, according to staff, to learn how to control it. After using RTP with Brent for four months, he now thinks through his aggressive episodes and chooses to make responsible decisions. He displays confidence and pride in his actions, and only two or three restraints have taken place over the four-month period. He is now able to go out of the BAC unit and read books to first graders on a weekly basis.

To date (November 1997), Tammy has four students who are making straight A's, only two physical restraints, and no time-outs over a three-month period. Her students are proud and very excited to be getting good grades. Prior to RTP, they said that they didn't care what grades they made, or even if they passed at all.

Jeff, another fifth grader, was very hyperactive and angry. He had spent three or more years in a BAC unit and had never been able to "make it" in the regular classrooms without being disruptive or dangerous. After RTP, he was able to be successful with other students in the regular classroom with few or no disruptions.

Organizational skills, communication skills, and social skills have all been dramatically improved for these students. They have demonstrated self-discipline through plan writing, by completing assigned tasks while keeping frustration levels low. Now the students in the BAC unit can recognize when they are becoming frustrated and can self-correct by taking a "chill-out." When students feel that they are back under control, they return to the task at hand. This skill prevents an escalation of behavior which could possibly lead to aggression and then a physical restraint. Instead of the teacher having to control by physical restraint, the students are now able themselves to bring that behavior under their own control.

School personnel, parents and grandparents have recognized social skills and self-control that were not present before the implementation of RTP. In the words of one BAC

unit student, "RTP makes me a better person and a successful role model."

In addition to the good results with students in the BAC
unit, I have also seen dramatic improvements with some
students who are in regular classrooms, as well as with
some students in resource and content mastery classes.

One student, Steve, was a fourth grader with a diagnosis
of ADHD and emotional disturbance when he was referred
to me for multiple discipline problems. He frequently ar-
gued with staff members and also intimidated teachers and
the principal. He refused to follow rules, refused to do
classwork, lied, and refused to take responsibility for his
own actions.

I introduced RTP to Steve one morning after training staff
the previous two days. I showed him the RTP cards and
plan sheets, and I explained to him how the process would
be implemented. His response was "I don't have to answer
any questions, and I will not write any plans." My response
was "You know what? You're right. You don't have to do any
of this. But if you want to be able to stay in the classroom,
the cafeteria, or out on the playground, you will be required to complete the plans. If you don't want to, that's
fine. You then will be choosing to be restricted from those
areas." This state of affairs did not please Steve at all. I started working with Steve at the beginning of the 1996–97
school year. During the school year, he wrote and revised
close to 30 plans. He chose to be sent home only twice during the year because of disruptions in the RTC room. He
spent a great deal of time in the restricted area out on the
playground, because he refused to follow the rules outside.
On the last day of the 1996–97 school year, he was still in
the restricted area on the playground. We saw Steve make
some drastic improvements, and most of his plans were
written at the beginning of the school year, with some
toward the end of May. Some months, he would only write
two or fewer plans. So we did see improvements in his willingness to follow rules.

However, Steve voiced his displeasure at having to write

plans, and he told staff and myself on numerous occasions that he would be going to a different elementary school next year, where he wouldn't have to "write those stupid plans anymore." Prior to the 1997–98 school year, Steve's mother informed us that she would be transferring Steve to another school in Amarillo because of housing difficulties. Prior to the 1997–98 school year, Steve's mother gave permission for the new school to continue to implement RTP. She did this without informing Steve. Prior to the beginning of school, I trained the staff at Steve's new school. They were supportive and more than willing to continue doing what had worked in the past.

On the first day at his new school, at 8:05 a.m., Steve was called into the principal's office. To his surprise, the principal and I met him and explained to him that nothing had changed as far as discipline: he would still be on RTP. Steve gave me a look that could have melted steel. The only comment that he made to me was "Do I still have to write those plans?" My response was "What do you think?" He replied back, "Not if I don't break the rules." He has not had to write any plans for four months now, and staff report no problems with his behavior. He did, however, have to start out in the restricted area at his new school, since he finished in the restricted area at his old school. At last report, the principal informed me that Steve liked it in the restricted area as long as a friend could play with him there.

Andy, a fifth grader, had a diagnosis of ADHD and emotional disturbance. He had a history of throwing desks, books, and any other objects that he could get his hands on. He threw the objects toward teachers and students. He was also verbally aggressive and had a history of excessive fighting with others on campus.

The staff met with Andy and his mother to outline RTP and what would take place if his disruptive behaviors continued. Andy wrote and revised many plans during the 1995–96 school year, and he was sent home on numerous occasions for disruptions in the RTC. His mother was always supportive with the staff and followed the plan at home as well. After approximately three months, we began to see wonderful results with Andy. He was placed on earn-all immediately after our meeting, but within those three months, he had earned back all of his classes and was no longer choosing to be disruptive or aggressive. After implementing RTP, he was in only one fight between November and the end of May. That fight took place off-campus.

The amazing thing about Andy's situation was that the following year, after being so successful at the elementary level, he went to the toughest middle school in Amarillo. That school refused to implement RTP or any ideas associated with it. At the middle school, he had only four office referrals the entire year! He no longer got into fights and was taking responsibility for his actions, even though staff were not using RTP. What an encouragement to know that, yes, RTP does work with tough kids even when there is no follow-through from the staff.

The final example comes from a seventh grader, Robert, who had a diagnosis of emotional disturbance and frequently interrupted classes by making noises, intimidating teachers, and basically not doing what was asked of him. In many cases, he would do the exact opposite of what staff instructed him to do. With RTP, Robert got the message very clearly that no more disruptions were allowed. Within two weeks, his behavior problems had decreased markedly, and the staff embraced RTP and tried it with other difficult students. I no longer received follow-up calls on his behavior.

The successes that have occurred in our classrooms give a true picture of what happens when we treat students with respect and consideration. When we treat them as individual living control systems, we truly find out what working with students is supposed to be like. Thanks to Ed, who taught me this process, to Tom Bourbon, who stayed up late helping me understand PCT, and to Tammy Mason, who believes in the process, her students, me, and especially Ed Ford. And thanks to all who truly believe that teaching children doesn't have to be a battle every day—if RTP and PCT are used.

Chapter 22
An Alternative for
Challenging Students

Bobbie Hodgins
Alternative Director/Educational Specialist
Choctaw Tribal Schools
Special Education Division
Philadelphia, Mississippi

Today, James is the first one to come bouncing through
the door, all smiles. He says good morning and sits down at
the dining table ready to eat breakfast. There are some
mornings when James is not as cheerful. Sometimes he is
hitting and yelling at the assistant, because he had to be literally picked up from inside his house screaming, not wanting to leave his collection of pennies. But he has greatly
improved from the way he was a year and a half ago.

James is 10 years old and is the most challenging student
we have had at our center. He has had the following diagnoses: fetal alcohol syndrome, complex seizure disorder,
mentally retarded, attention deficit disorder, communication deficits, and severe behavior problems. One might
think that our facility is for severely disabled students, but
our program was begun four years ago to serve youth with
severe emotional and behavioral problems in lieu of residential placement. James was placed at the center a year
ago because of his severe behavior problems in the elementary school setting. The behaviors displayed included
running down the hall, taking his clothes off in the bath-
room, and defecating at random throughout the building.

Several meetings had been held to discuss what would
be a more appropriate setting in which James could func-

tion in a less disruptive manner. He was assigned to us temporarily with a shortened school day until other options were explored. His grandmother, who is his guardian, refused to consider another placement, wanting him to remain with us. As a result, permanent placement was established in our center.

This decision required significant changes in the operation of the center. A full-time assistant, Dan Isaac, was hired to work with James one-on-one. Dan, a teacher's assistant, had been working in one of the special ed classes at our elementary school where James was first placed. Dan became a critical part of James' treatment plan. He facilitated James' transition from isolation to small group behavior. Behavior modification was found to be totally ineffective in helping James learn to control his behavior.

I had first been introduced to RTP at a conference and through the first edition of this book. I had already initiated the program with all of our students, with a great deal of success. We had watched our students take on more and more responsibility by learning to think for themselves and deal with others in a more respectful way. We decided to use RTP with James, believing that he was capable of being responsible for his actions and thinking for himself.

When James disrupted, it was always a *major* disruption, and so we would use a time-out room; if we sent him to the RTC, he would only continue to disrupt there, which would keep that room from functioning as it should. The time-out room is a small, padded room—more like a closet—with a window. Dan would escort James to the room and stay with him until James was calm enough to answer questions. He asked James the responsible thinking questions, which helped James think about what he was doing and whether he was willing to take responsibility for his actions. Dan would help him work through each episode, once James was calm. The following is a typical dialogue between Dan and James:

Dan (in a soft, calm, curious manner): James, what did you do to Leisa? (Leisa Bridges is the special ed teacher who works with the group that James is in.)

James: Hit.

Dan (using simple, easy-to-understand phrases): Is it OK to hit Miss Leisa? (The students refer to their teacher as "Miss Leisa" or "Leisa.")

James: No.

Dan (repeating the question using a different phrase to assure commitment): Was that the thing to do?

James: No.

Dan: What are you going to tell Leisa? (Since detailed or written plan making is too sophisticated for James, Dan helps to direct his thinking, but James decides how he is going to deal with her and what he is going to say.)

James: Won't hit again.

Dan (making sure that James is calm enough to re-enter the group): Are you ready to go back to the group?

James: Yes.

Dan (checking to see whether James remembers what he has planned to do): What will you say to Leisa?

James: I'm sorry.

Dan (checking to see whether James is still committed to and remembers his plan): And what are you going to say to Leisa?

James: Won't hit again. (James then returns to the group after he has given his apology to Leisa.)

When James first came to our center, he was going to the time-out up to eight times a day. Soon, that decreased to four or five times a day, then to three or four times a week. At the end of the school year, he went for three weeks without a disruption. If he hit his teacher, say on the arm, when he would return, he would go over to her, gently stroke her arm where he had slapped her, and then often kiss where he had slapped her. Often, he would hug the teacher. Thus, by the end of the school year, James had shown remarkable improvement. Dan was able to draw his attention at the first indication of a disruption by just asking the question, "James, what are you doing?" Nothing else was needed. James would usually respond by settling down. It was no longer necessary for him to leave the small group setting and go through the entire process. James then went home for his summer vacation.

At the beginning of the second year, James' disruptions were about where he was halfway through his first year. The running through the halls, defecating at random, and taking off his clothes were no more. He could start his day at his own desk, rather than having to share a table with Dan. His ability to keep at a task increased from five to 15 minutes. Although his seizure disorder continued to present challenges to his ability to think and act responsibly, constant use of the process has helped him to continue to improve. Due to his continued successes, James is allowed to participate in activities, such as going to the gym and the library, which would have been unthinkable a year earlier.

The RTP program has proven highly successful in helping all of our students, but especially James and others who have similar disabilities. Gone are all the reinforcement-type programs which have proven ineffective. No longer do we believe those who tell us that these students cannot tell the difference between right and wrong. RTP has proved to be a godsend! The basic principles this process operates upon, namely teaching children to think for themselves and to control their own experiences, rather than our trying to control what we see them doing, are applicable to all human interactions. Personal responsibility developed by children through RTP allows them to develop skills that will prepare them to experience success in other relationships outside the classroom. In fact, the principles can easily be transferred to staff supervision and personal relationships.

I want to give a special thanks to Chief Phillip Martin, who supported my documentation of these positive experiences. Also, I thank James' guardian for allowing this publication. I appreciate her confidence in our ability to help James develop a plan to meet his special needs. And a very special thanks to all of my staff, who work so hard to help our children think and plan their way toward being responsible students.

Chapter 23
Juvenile Corrections and RTP:
How It Works at
Catalina Mountain School

Bill Lackman
RTC Teacher
Catalina Mountain School, Tucson
Arizona Department of Juvenile Corrections

I first met Ed Ford in 1995, when he was hired as a consultant by the Arizona Department of Juvenile Corrections. After surveying our educational system, Ed chose Catalina Mountain School (CMS) in Tucson, a maximum security facility for juveniles, as the location in which to pilot his responsible thinking process (RTP) in a juvenile corrections setting. This had never before been attempted, so it was an intriguing experiment for all of us, and a wonderful opportunity to share our findings with other professionals in juvenile corrections. I began to understand that if our project were successful, we could help enormously across the country by serving as a viable model for others who serve adjudicated, neglected, and delinquent youth.

Soon after Ed had made his first visit to CMS to meet and speak with the faculty, I was asked to leave my position as an instructor in another program to structure and operate the CMS responsible thinking classroom (RTC). I was at first hesitant; however, this opportunity was too good to ignore. Sonia Vernon, assistant principal at CMS, was designated to act as RTP Administrator, and we began to work together to decide where and how to begin.

We knew that training the faculty was the next logical step, so Ed returned to CMS. All faculty members were trained in the use of RTP and were provided with a basic understanding of PCT during scheduled in-service prior to implementation, and Ed and I spent time together discussing how the RTC should be arranged and operated. Once we were all adequately grounded in RTP and had a firm understanding of our roles as faculty members and administrators beginning this new process, we were ready to present the project to the facility administrators, managers, housing unit staff, and students. We accomplished this by meeting with individual administrators, attending and reporting progress and concerns at management team and faculty meetings, and giving presentations to each housing unit's staff and students. At every point, we encouraged questions and communication. Procedural guidelines for RTP were established and discussed, and expectations of all parties were outlined prior to implementation.

In addition to securing administrative support, placing the right people in key positions, and insuring that sufficient training occurs, there are other critical elements which need to be put in place in order to make implementing RTP as smooth a process as possible. Understanding that adaptations in the program structure will occur, it is still helpful to identify and produce as much of the organizational structure as possible in the beginning. For example, I found it very useful to produce a flow chart (shown on page 174) tracking a student through the RTC experience. This chart enables a more immediate understanding of the process by both staff and students.

Creating linkages across the facility, whenever possible, helps to build the infrastructure that can support your efforts over the long term. At CMS, establishing these linkages helped to lead toward a more team-based approach to addressing youth behavior in the school setting. I began to furnish each housing unit lead teacher with a weekly feedback form indicating which students attended RTC during that week and how many visits they made (whether through making improper choices leading to RTC referral or on a

RTC Flow Chart

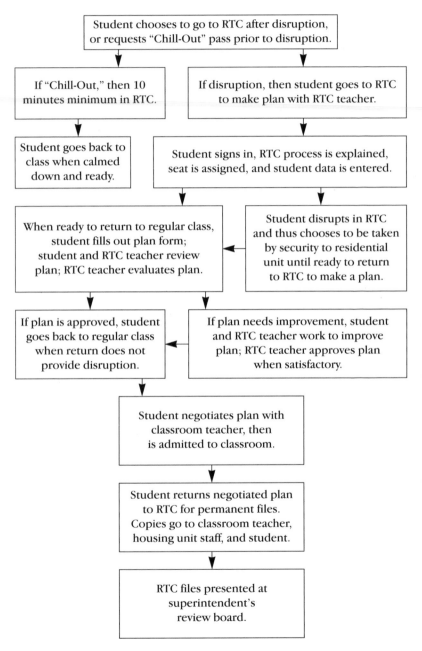

Student chooses to go to RTC after disruption, or requests "Chill-Out" pass prior to disruption.

If "Chill-Out," then 10 minutes minimum in RTC.

If disruption, then student goes to RTC to make plan with RTC teacher.

Student goes back to class when calmed down and ready.

Student signs in, RTC process is explained, seat is assigned, and student data is entered.

When ready to return to regular class, student fills out plan form; student and RTC teacher review plan; RTC teacher evaluates plan.

Student disrupts in RTC and thus chooses to be taken by security to residential unit until ready to return to RTC to make a plan.

If plan is approved, student goes back to regular class when return does not provide disruption.

If plan needs improvement, student and RTC teacher work to improve plan; RTC teacher approves plan when satisfactory.

Student negotiates plan with classroom teacher, then is admitted to classroom.

Student returns negotiated plan to RTC for permanent files. Copies go to classroom teacher, housing unit staff, and student.

RTC files presented at superintendent's review board.

"Chill-Out" pass (time-out) basis. (A sample pass is shown at the end of this chapter.) Once we began to transfer RTP into the housing units, both education and housing unit staff were able to have a more global perspective on each youth's conduct in multiple settings. I hope to reach the point soon where each youth referred to the RTC must present his plan(s) to his housing unit Multidisciplinary (Treatment) Team for final approval and follow-up. This occurs sometimes now, but not with the consistency I wish to see. Although the connection between education and housing units is not yet complete, I am certain that we will make steady improvement through continued training and support, and maintaining our shared vision that responsible thinking promotes success.

As a result of creating a link with our Crisis Management Team (CMT), both the security and education departments have begun to share data through the RTC. In building the RTC in the early stages, I looked for ways to measure effectiveness of the program and what impact RTP might have on our facility. I established baselines in a number of different areas, including a comparison of the total number of security calls in both education and housing units. Comparing the year prior to implementation to the first year following implementation shows a 52% reduction in security calls to education and a 42% reduction in security calls to housing units. The difference can be heard and seen: classrooms and housing units are quieter and more effective. The linkage between education and CMT has thus yielded a new way of looking at what we do and how we do it, and it has spurred further interest in assessing this data. For example, I now send three copies of my RTC monthly report to the CMT for their use. And 11 other persons in various departments receive copies, as well.

By using a portion of the monthly report as an educational evaluation tool, we can identify or confirm those students having the most difficulty in their classrooms. This information is available weekly in our student study team, but looking at the monthly trend focuses on the more pro-

550555

tracted cases. In the tables below, for example, you will see that a very small number of students accounted for a significant number of RTC visits in two successive months.

Student RTC Attendance, CTM, September 1997

Number of Students	Number of RTC Visits
1 *	9
1 *	8
2 *	7
2 *	5
2	4
2	3
11	2
23	1
Total 44	Total 100

Total population: 138.
Number choosing to follow rules and not attend RTC: 94.
Percentage choosing to follow rules and not attend RTC: 68%.
Students with asterisks (*) accounted for 41% of monthly RTC attendance.

Student RTC Attendance, CTM, October 1997

Number of Students	Number of RTC Visits
1 *	7
2 *	6
2 *	5
3 *	4
1	3
11	2
29	1
Total 49	Total 95

Total population: 140.
Number choosing to follow rules and not attend RTC: 91.

Percentage choosing to follow rules and not attend RTC: 65%.

Students with asterisks (*) accounted for 43% of monthly RTC attendance.

It is interesting to note that at every location where RTP has been implemented, a "J-curve" effect, as shown in the tables above, has been demonstrated. That is, a relatively small number of students account for a large portion of total disruptions. To understand that the most troubled children can be identified for more intensive treatment is a very enabling characteristic of RTP.

Sharing information such as this with all who have interactions with these students can lead to more cohesive, and therefore more effective, treatment for the students. One particularly interesting case involved Frankie. His frustration was clearly observable in all of his classes. Even though he was intelligent and talented, he was highly disruptive, abusive, and uninterested in anything to do with academics. Consequently, Frankie chose to attend the RTC on an almost constant basis over a period of a couple of months. At first openly defiant, Frankie began to respond appropriately to questioning and to see that his choices were starting to cost too much. This occurred after the first month of frequent attendance. Through a process of practicing his plan in school and exploratory conversation in the RTC, he began to develop an idea of what he wanted. He soon found an opportunity to try his idea, and he never looked back. He learned how to cook in our food service program, and when I last heard, he was working as a chef at a local resort. He also served as RTC monitor for his housing unit while at CMS, and his difficulties in the classroom virtually disappeared.

I have seen another positive effect of disseminating this data throughout the facility. Kids are naturally drawn to visual information, and I have observed that our students are paying increasingly more attention to the graphs and charts I produce for the RTC monthly report. Several are exhibited in the RTC, and not a day goes by without students commenting on them. This in turn has engendered a competitive spirit among the students, and they consistently ask me, "Who has the most RTC's this month, Mr. Lackman?" Housing units have also responded well by having one or more students act as RTC monitors. That is, these students track who attended the RTC from their housing unit each week, and how many times they attended. This has been a very supportive action and has helped to strengthen RTP at CMS by increasing the awareness of the process among the more responsible students.

We have come a long way in establishing an effective discipline program at CMS since we first implemented RTP in August 1996. It has been difficult and frustrating at times, but the results we have observed have been worth every bit of the effort. The classroom environment has been improved for everyone, with significantly fewer disruptions. Expectations are clear for everyone. We have established key linkages across the facility and are continuing to nurture them, as well as creating others. Each RTC monthly and annual report adds to our unique and functional database, and I continue to look for productive ways to use the information and to make it accessible to others. What has been most gratifying, however, is observing how RTP has helped us build better relationships with our students, and how they have more frequently chosen to think responsibly.

I look forward to improving RTP at CMS during this next year, and I plan to emphasize additional training and connections across the facility. An immediate goal is to strengthen the link between RTP and our Multidisciplinary (Treatment) Teams. This will enhance the wrap-around care philosophy of the Arizona Department of Juvenile Corrections. A second emphasis will be directed toward sharing this successful model with the other schools in our Department. A program which yields such positive results needs to be shared.

I would like to acknowledge the wonderful cooperation

and support of the following persons: Mr. Dave Gaspar, Deputy Director, Arizona Department of Juvenile Corrections; Mr. Tom Turos, Superintendent, CMS; Mr. Alan Mielke, Principal, CMS; and Ms. Sonia Vernon, Assistant Principal, CMS.

```
                        "Chill-Out"
                          Pass

    This pass allows you to use the Responsible Thinking
Classroom (RTC) if you find yourself getting angry and
you need time to "chill-out" for a reasonable period
of time in a safe and more restricted area.  When you
want to return to regular programming, you and your
RTC teacher will determine if and when you are ready.
This pass should be given to the RTC teacher.  The
pass is given only to those who request its use prior
to disruptive behavior or as part of making a plan
with the RTC teacher.


Name _____ K# _____ Housing Unit _____


Referring Teacher _____ Date _____


Time student asked to leave _____ Arrived RTC _____


Returned to Regular Class _____ Housing Unit _____


Other _____ CMT Called: Yes ____ No ____


Additional Comments:
```

Chapter 24
Creating Community
via Classroom Discussions

LeEdna Custer-Knight
School Psychologist
Clarendon Elementary School
Osborn School District
Phoenix, Arizona

Discipline resides within the child. The word is derived from a Latin root meaning "to grasp." No amount of points, smiley faces, gifts, or bribes can create a disciplined child. Nor can any amount of yelling, hitting, or punishment.

Ed Ford's application of perceptual control theory via the responsible thinking process is the first discipline program to acknowledge children as self-controlling by nature and to focus on a process that does not promote the illusion that they are controlled by other people. His questioning process provides a cognitive structure through which possible actions can be screened to determine if their unintended results would be in conflict with higher-level goals. (I.e., "I want to shove Joey. If I shove, I will be choosing to go to the RTC and work on a plan. I will miss recess. I want to be outside more than I want to shove.") This process actually results in more choice and a clearer understanding of any possible conflicts. Therefore, it is easy to understand why the program's success was dramatic.

At Clarendon, we saw dramatic results within four months. As our children began to think and act more responsibly, our school became a much more peaceful place. Having the time to reflect, I began to question the ultimate goal of any "discipline program." Ed Ford says (and I must admit I agree) that RTP aims to teach children how to achieve their goals without violating the rights of others. However, as I reviewed the process, I became increasingly uncomfortable with the second question of the questioning process, "What's the rule?" Implicit in that question is the concept that "the rule" is the guideline for choices. While at a pragmatic level this might be true—children must learn to abide by the standards of where they are to be successful—it is not the ultimate goal of RTP to create rule-bound children who make choices based on extrinsic guidelines. Creating conditions where a child considers the rights of others before acting implies that the child believes violating the rights of others is not acceptable. Not acceptable—why?

Were our students choosing not to violate the rights of others because it was a "rule," or because they had developed an internal set of standards to guide their choices? At best, their choices were reflecting internalized standards; at worst, their choices were only reflecting referencing an immediate higher-level goal (i.e., "I want to stay outside and play during recess more than I want to hit Joey."). The reality was probably somewhere in between.

Often, in meeting with teachers to discuss a child whose actions were of concern, I would hear descriptions of acts that were demeaning, hurtful, or in some manner diminished another. While RTP had greatly diminished serious violations such as assaults, fighting, and disruptions during class, I was concerned that a significant number of children did not seem able, or perhaps willing, to screen choices in terms other than the immediate impact on their lives.

A critical component of Ed's process is creating quality time: in homes, one-on-one; and in schools, through student discussions. (See Chapter 6.) Unfortunately, I have found that educators often underestimate the significance of these discussions. Maria Montessori knew decades ago what current learning theory espouses, that the most successful learning is experiential. When discussing a child's language development, Ed states that a child's concept of a word comes from her experience with it. For example, initially the concept of mama is tied solely to the child's mother. The child's experiences with her mother create a unique conceptual understanding of mama. As the child grows, this conceptual understanding broadens to include experiences with other mothers and finally to the generalized concept of mama or mother as a female parent. If we accept that in order to understand the concepts of language, one must experience them, is it not logical to acknowledge that in order to comprehend the concepts and benefits of mutual respect and caring, a child must first experience them and perceive them as beneficial? Once experienced and perceived as beneficial, would there not be a high probability of integrating those concepts within the individual's hierarchy of goals? If so, the likely result would be that an absence of mutual respect and caring would create an error signal within the child, who would then act to correct it. The need for extrinsic "rules" would then greatly diminish.

Student discussions are the ideal setting for "being there" experiences of mutual respect and caring. As Ed has stated, it is the job of the educator to maintain a fair, noncritical climate where children are taught via experience to respect the words of others. My experience at Clarendon and then at other schools involved with RTP has been that many teachers fail to consistently implement this part of the process. While the program can appear effective without student discussions, it is rarely as efficient as when the discussions are held.

As stated earlier, I had become increasingly uncomfortable with the word "rule" and had gradually become aware that many staff members of our school were not committed to regularly scheduled student discussions. I saw two potential benefits to student discussions. First, by experience, the students could learn to respect others while interacting and reflecting on what was being discussed. Second, discussions could allow students to experience various social skills and character attributes likely to result in the development of mutual respect and caring.

I believe by age 9 or 10 (actually often much, much earlier) children have developed internal standards and values. However, as a result of many parents working at least one full-time job, if not more, parents are often harried and might not spend a great deal of time sharing their standards with their children. Also, given many families' diminished participation in organized religion, civic causes, and/or volunteerism, children often miss valuable opportunities to experience empathy, caring, and the concept of service to others. Add to this the significant effect of substance abuse and violence that many families experience, and there is little wonder why children often have no organized, cohesive, easily accessed, and articulated internal standards through which to readily screen their actions. So actions might, if screened for conflict at all, be internally screened for immediate negative consequences only.

To create a perceived need for such an internal system through questioning became my challenge. In reviewing how, in staff and student discussions, our school community developed the rules we now live by, I remembered that we began with the simple question, "What rules do you think our school needs and why?" We had rather quickly arrived at a reasonable list of rules with which students, staff, and parents could agree to live.

I was sure the answer to this challenge had to be simple. I began a new series of discussions with a fifth grade class by asking, "What would the perfect school look like, sound like, and feel like?" (We first established that there were no wrong or right answers, and criticism was not allowed.) Students were not only willing but eager to share their "perfect school" fantasies. "It would feel safe." "You wouldn't hear name calling." "No teachers yelling." "No stealing." "No hitting." Then I asked, "What would I hear?" "Laughing." "Quiet." "Teachers being nice." "Compliments." "And how would you feel there?" "Happy." "Excited." "Not bored." "Not scared." "Not angry." "OK, what would the perfect class look like, feel like, sound like?" Again, the students seemed to know exactly what their concept of the perfect class was and aptly described it. "No put downs." "People saying kind things." "No stealing." "No one hurting anyone with words." "No hitting." "No teachers yelling." "No homework." I asked, "What would I see and hear?" "People talking quietly." "The teacher teaching." "Students working together." "Sometimes laughing." "People helping." "People sharing." And, "How would you feel there?" "Happy." "Not bored." "Safe." "Excited." "Good." "Like school was cool." I then asked, "What do you think the perfect member of this class would sound like and feel like, and what would I see him or her doing?" "He wouldn't take things too seriously." "She would be kind." "He wouldn't steal or lie." "You could trust him." "She would help out." "She would be cooperative." "Hey, you know, the guy could take a joke, you know, and wouldn't get all hot." "Not too serious." "He would do something if he said he would." "You could count on her." "She would want to learn." "She would help in a group." "He wouldn't quit." "He wouldn't always be doing stupid stuff." "No interrupting."

I or the teacher wrote the comments on large sheets of paper titled "Perfect School," "Perfect Class," and "Perfect Member." Then we looked over the comments. When we came to the sheet regarding the perfect member of this class, after reviewing the comments, I asked, "Do any of these seem similar? Which ones? Do you think there is one word that might describe those that are similar?" And so, a list of desirable attributes came to be. Many were student-generated; some I generated (as descriptors of the students' statements, only). I then asked if they would be interested in trying to create "the ideal class" this year. They enthusiastically said yes. I asked if they would like to meet weekly and talk about these attributes and how they felt things were going. Again, a unanimous yes. We talked about the word "community," what it meant, and would they commit to trying to create their ideal learning community. They all agreed to commit to the effort. I was not surprised to find children who wanted the opportunity to meet weekly and express their opinions, without criticism, and to be given unconditional regard. Having facilitated group counseling for many years and student discussions for several, I know children often have few opportunities to freely express themselves without fear of reprisal, mocking, or critique, both well-intended and not. However, I was truly shocked by the unanimity to go for it, work and all. We labeled our overall task "Creating Community."

An unanticipated benefit of this process that occurred after making the commitment to create community was that I found myself no longer asking, "What's the rule?" To students in this class, I could ask, "What are you doing?" and then, "Are you living your commitment?" No longer was their reference extrinsic.

Where did this journey take us? Within a month, I knew these kids were serious. Each week, we began our discussions with a quick check-in on how we were doing, and then we discussed a specific character attribute, again with the students telling me what it meant, what it would look like, sound like, feel like, and giving examples of when they needed to use it.

Who were we? While the class had a strong core of four or five gifted students, it also had a larger group of English-as-a-second-language students (several required peer translators during the discussions, yet still were active participants and accepted by their peers) and several special education students who were receiving Learning Disability Resource services and were concurrently diagnosed as ADHD (two took no medication; one child had been in a self-contained program for children with emotional disabilities three years before). We were a diverse population, truly reflective of our school's multicultural urban community.

What happened? I was continually amazed by the desire these students had to create their "ideal," even when it meant personal change and effort. A real marker occurred when Tom Bourbon visited our school to observe and evaluate our application of perceptual control theory. He attended student discussions. I explained his presence as an observer to the class and asked if it was OK for him to stay. No objections. In an attempt to give Tom a snapshot of what we had been doing, I stated that our goal in the fall had been to create the "Ideal Class." We discussed what that would look like, sound like, feel like. I then asked each student to assess where they perceived the class to be in reference to their "ideal" by rating it from 1 to 10, 1 being not there at all and 10 being perfect alignment. I knew we had succeeded in empowering the students in recognition that they were self-controlling when they began discussing their desire to each create their own rating scale (i.e., 1% to 100%, A to Z, Z to A, etc.). I quickly agreed to free use of any scale, as long as they explained its meaning. I also requested that they support their rating with examples of what they had seen, heard, or felt in given situations. I was truly surprised when the lowest rating anyone (including the "tough guys") gave the class in meeting "their ideal" was B or 90%, with many stating "we're there" and being able to cite detailed examples of peers demonstrating specific character attributes (i.e., "Jimmy demonstrated integrity when he found Maria's money and he gave it to her instead of keeping it.").

This initial dive into waters which for me were previously uncharted was an amazing experience. This first class was incredible; they taught me much that other classes continue to affirm. They challenged and then shattered many of my preconceived opinions about our children, and they affirmed a few of my most optimistic beliefs. I must acknowledge what an incredible gift I was given by these children, who willingly gave me access to their internal worlds. Also, most significant is Alicia Behrens, their very courageous, gifted teacher, who engages her charges with incredible instructional practices and acceptance. She trusted me enough to take the dive, too!

Since my first experience in Creating Community, I have met with many more classes. Not all have been as successful as the first. The true key seems not to be the mix of students, but rather the day-to-day commitment of staff to model what we believe and to truly support student choice (within the limits of safety and respect for others' rights). There appears to be great commonality as to what children perceive as an ideal (error-free) environment. Paramount, after safety, appears to be the freedom to be self-controlling without fear of punishment or criticism, and to be given unconditional acceptance and regard. While the desire for safety and acceptance are not surprising, what has continued to astonish me is the discovery of children's willingness to do the hard work of keeping commitments and making personal changes in order to achieve their ideal, and their ability to successfully create a highly functional community. It appears to me that Bill Powers, whose genius I never questioned, is very close to an accurate explanation of the nature of life as a hierarchy of control systems acting to correct error.

To be freely self-controlling has been a goal for which I have repeatedly seen children willing to subordinate other high-level goals (i.e., control of others via intimidation, the freedom of impulsivity, or unharnessed aggression). I am also amazed by how often we all appear to want the same thing: to be part of a community that functions with the recognition of individual autonomy and the need to respect the rights of others. We appear, at least as children, to have a strong sense of what is called "character" and to see it as valuable. The big question remaining is how to move from small individual classrooms to larger and larger groups who deeply commit to creating community.

Chapter 25
Working with Parents

Joseph Sierzenga
Former Principal
Morrice Elementary School
Morrice, Michigan

As an administrator, my role in RTP is to drive the program. But what exactly does that mean? To me, it means that administrators must find methods that encourage all members of the school community to become a part of the process. Other chapters in this book address interactions of students, teachers, and administrators within the physical structure of the school. In this chapter, I provide ideas on expanding the process into the school community, dealing with issues such as student plans, RTC disruptions, acts of physical violence, and homework.

Parents are critical to the success of RTP. They can provide crucial support for a beginning program and can fight to save RTP if school budgets reduce programs or call for the elimination of RTP. For this to happen, parents *must* perceive RTP as valuable. Recently, a colleague of mine gave an RTP program update to our Board of Education. During the presentation, several Board members began to question the validity and success of RTP. They were considering the possibility of eliminating the program altogether, district-wide. In the audience that night were several elementary school teachers and parents. Although the discussion focused on RTP at the secondary level, several of those teachers and parents voiced their support for the program. We heard comments such as these: "For the first time in my children's education, I am being asked what I want." "We work as a team in solving problems." "I finally know what my child is doing and how I can help in the process." "In solving problems, we do not spend time trying to blame each other." "I wish they had this when I was in school." "I can finally teach." I then realized that these comments were evidence that the teachers and parents were quite vigorously controlling for the perception of RTP continuing in our district, showing that we have passed the implementation stage. We can now set our sights on becoming certified. We had been careful to let our intentions regarding implementation of RTP be known in advance so that both teachers and parents would have ample opportunity to develop support for the program.

In the area of student plans, I have found that almost all parents want to know how their children are doing and, more importantly, want to know how they can help in the educational process. Parents perceive the school as part of their attempts to control their own perceptions related to raising and educating their children. Failure to acknowledge this fact can make the school—including RTP—a disturbance opposed by the parents. Parent involvement in student plan-making should be treated as a part of the process. Upon initial contact with parents, the RTC teacher should gather information about what the parents feel they need to know. Issues such as types of disruptions, frequency of visits to the RTC, and how the parents see themselves assisting in this process can be discussed. Based on the initial conversation, the RTC teacher might recommend that the principal make a follow-up call to the parents to discuss RTP, its operation at the school, and possible ways the parents could assist in this process. The center of the discussion always should be on *what they want for their children*, and the principal's role should be to find common ground upon which to build a relationship to assist the process.

Involving parents should *not* be viewed as an attempt to shift the responsibility of dealing with school disruptions to the home. Some administrators and teachers claim to have a non-coercive school environment and then enlist the services of parents to administer rewards and selected punishments. Instead, our attempts to involve parents are invitational: we ask parents to support the RTP process, we discuss the underlying intent of rules, and we make connections between school rules, home rules, and community rules. Our focus is not on compliance to rules, but on the necessity of having certain agreed-upon conditions to allow people to work together.

In some situations, the involvement of parents can compound a problem. For example, an abusive parent administering corporal punishment places a student in a difficult situation and creates negative perceptions of RTP. In cases where abuse is suspected, I work with the students to find acceptable alternatives to the parents. In those cases, the students are asked if they can identify school staff who would be willing to act as their parents during the school day. I have been honored to have been selected as a surrogate parent in several situations requiring restricted participation of true parents. In each case, the student and I discuss what it means to be part of a family, how a family works together, and how a family should resolve problems. With the student and myself looking at a photograph of my family, I ask questions such as these:

- What do you think it means to be part of my family?
- Do you feel you should follow the same rules as my children at home?
- Should my expectations be the same for you as they are for my children at home?
- How do you think we handle problems at home?
- If my children have problems, what do you think they do?
- Would you like to know my expectations for my children?
- Are you still willing to be a part of my family?

The student and I then develop a plan or agreement that addresses the conditions of this new arrangement. The student's parents are informed that their child will be dealing directly with the building administrator, and they are asked if they are willing to work with me. Information concerning their child's behavior is communicated to the parents by me on a need-to-know basis. When dealing with difficult parents, I usually ask the following questions:

• What do you want for your child?
• How do you want your child to perceive you?
• What type of relationship do you want to have with your child?
• What type of relationship do you think your child wants to have with you?
• Is what you're currently doing developing the type of relationship you want?
• How do you perceive the school in relation to this problem?
• What do you want to do now?
• Are you willing to work with me on dealing with these issues at school?

Through this process, I attempt to develop a different concept of family, without undermining the existing parent/child relationship. There is no issue of right vs. wrong, but an exploration of positive alternatives. In the end, the students create their own concepts of family based on their own experiences, not on ours.

With regard to RTC disruptions and acts of physical violence, the principal is often placed in situations with conflicts among RTP, parent preferences, school board policies, and community perceptions. In such situations, I have always attempted to gain support from parents by communicating our intentions and explaining the parents' role *before* a problem arises that requires action on their part. Again, the question "What do you want for your child?" is discussed in relation to RTP, and through this discussion we decide what we need to do together to achieve parental goals. Typically, parents send their child to school and then control for unrelated perceptions until the school day is over. A sudden unexpected call from the school requesting a parent to suddenly control for other perceptions, such as picking up a child, makes the school a disturbance with regard to the perceptions currently being controlled by the parent (such as earning money, shopping, or taking care of an ill relative). Such disturbances are often opposed by the parents, and the focus usually shifts from helping the students in making responsible choices to the school's inability to control the student.

In our school, we have implemented a simple process that adds the necessary degrees of freedom allowing everyone to control their perceptions relative to everyone's responsibilities in RTP. The following process is used for students who have been involved in an RTC disruption or an act of physical violence for the first time:

1. I conduct a conference with the student and ask the following questions:

• What is the rule concerning RTC disruptions/acts of physical violence?

• Do you think this is a good rule?

• What would happen if we did not have this rule?

• Were you asked the RTP questions?

• What was your choice?

• What do we need to do now?

• Would you like to talk to your parents or would you like me to? (If the student wants to call and speak on his own behalf, we usually role-play the phone call beforehand.)

2. The parents are notified by phone of their child's behavior. We review the RTP process and develop a plan that addresses the action required by the parents if their child chooses again to disrupt in the RTC or to commit an act of physical violence.

3. The student is placed in an in-school suspension situation until the parents provide us with the name(s) and phone number(s) of the person(s) responsible for picking up the student.

4. The student develops a plan with me to return to the RTC, and a follow-up phone call is made to the parents, thanking them for their support. Sometimes an additional conference is required to discuss RTP with the parents.

When a child is involved in an RTC disruption or an act

of physical violence a second time, we follow the agreed-upon plan previously developed. What this usually means is that I will conduct a conference with the student. The student and I will call the responsible person identified by the plan to pick up the student, who will remain at home until willing to work with us. When the student is ready to work with us, I will conduct a conference with the student and parents to negotiate the conditions of re-entry to school. The student returns to the RTC and, when ready, begins to develop a plan to return to class. What once was a difficult situation for both the parent and administrator is now an orchestrated sequence of events with the child solely responsible for the intended and unintended consequences of his behavior.

Student homework is another situation where we enlist the services of the parents. In my experience, most parents are more than willing to be part of the education of their children. The unfortunate fact is that educators have not done an adequate job of communicating, in specific terms, exactly how parents can help. Assignments that are sent home often place parents in situations that pit them against their children. Many family arguments during the school year center around children's unwillingness to complete homework assignments. The endless games of control and counter-control among teachers, parents, and students usually result in the parents faulting the school or questioning the classroom teachers' capabilities. On the other hand, some teachers perceive parents as not caring about the educational needs of the classroom and the importance of learning. The result of this interaction tends to let students off the hook, not completing assignments, as parents and teachers argue about who is not being responsible.

The process I have developed and have found successful is called Learning Journal Planning. I attempt to define and obtain commitment on the roles and responsibilities of parents, classroom teachers, students, and building principals. This process may be initiated by a student, teacher, or parent. Once initiated, it becomes the responsibility of the principal to organize, facilitate, and monitor the development and implementation of the Learning Journal Plan.

The first step is to obtain commitments from all persons who are involved. Obtaining commitments is the responsibility of the administrator driving the program. To parents becoming part of this process, I ask the following questions:

- What type of student do you want your child to be?
- Do you believe that your child should complete school assignments?
- What are the standards at home concerning homework assignments?
- What do you think the standards concerning homework are at school?
- Do we share similar standards concerning homework assignments?
- In what way do our standards differ?
- Are you satisfied with how things are going?
- Are you willing to develop a plan with your child and your child's classroom teachers to make it better?
- When is a convenient time to develop this plan?

I have found that most parents are willing to be part of a process that is monitored on a daily basis by classroom teachers and on a weekly basis by the building principal. A few parents are not willing to commit to the development of a comprehensive plan. In such situations, I probe to find out exactly how far they are willing to go, and I attempt to develop a plan within those parameters. I am willing to work with parents where they are and expand what we do as they become able and committed to handling more. In extreme cases, where the parents have no interest in assisting their child on homework issues, I would simply ask them to sign a prepared letter stating that they are not interested in becoming part of the educational process of their child, and that they understand the school is making every attempt to educate their child without parental support at home. If at any time they wish to re-evaluate their decision, the building principal will be more than happy to assist them in developing a Learning Journal Plan. During the past four years of working with parents on homework issues, I have never had parents unwilling to become part of this process; however, I have had several parents request termination of the Learning Journal Plan. Their conclusion was that they were not as interested as they had perceived themselves to be, and that the school would just have to do the best it can. This process protects the integrity of the classroom and the teacher who is responsible for the learning that takes place there. (See, in Chapter 10, how I worked with a classroom teacher and her students to develop the discipline of study.)

In closing, there is one final point that I would like to make about working with parents. Typically, parents do not perceive me as Joe Sierzenga, the person, but rather as the embodiment of their experiences defining the concept of "principal." As Ed Ford has stated, "It's how a person perceives you that determines how they deal with you." I believe it is important to spend time with parents gathering information about how they perceive "school," "principal," and "teacher." I ask questions such as these:

• When you think of the word "school," what memories come to mind?

• What did you like about your school experiences?

• During your schooling, is there a period that you disliked?

• What type of school would you wish for your children?

• If you could change one aspect of your schooling, what would it be?

• Who was your favorite building principal?

• What qualities separated this person from other building principals?

• How do you perceive me as your child's building principal?

• When you were in school, how did the building principals assist you in solving problems?

• If you could make one recommendation to building principals based on your experiences in school, what would it be?

• When you were in school, were you ever sent to building principals for disciplinary action?

• What did they do well? What do you think they could have done differently?

• Do you understand the RTP program?

• How does it fit with your school experiences?

• What would you like for your child?

• Are you willing to work with us in the RTP program to get what you want?

Through these discussions, I attempt to develop working relationships with parents. My goal is to have them perceive me as Joe Sierzenga, the person, not as the category "building principal." I also attempt to highlight the points where RTP is consistent with their current beliefs and with what they wanted for themselves when they were in school. The focus is always on the areas we have in common and on where the parents' current perceptions of school might be inaccurate. The question "Is that what we do here?" works in the same way as the question "What are you doing?" that we ask our students. The intent is to focus thinking on what is currently being done, not on past experiences.

Parents do the best they can in the situations in which they find themselves. We try to help them find ways of controlling their perceptions relative to being a good parent, while allowing us to control our perceptions of what it means to be educators.

Chapter 26
RTP and the School Bus Driver

Rex C. Squires
Transportation Director
Blaine County School District #61
Hailey, Idaho

How We Got Started

The school environment doesn't exist only in the class-room—it starts with that first step onto the school bus in the early morning dark near the student's home. The ride to school might be uneventful and, yes, even boring. But what happens when something different occurs? What about that new student who has never ridden a bus before in this school district? How will that student behave on a new bus and at a new school?

The Blaine County School District has been working with Ed Ford for several years. After the first couple of years, the district realized that only the school personnel (main-ly administrators and teachers) had been trained to use RTP. Many of the problems that occurred within the district didn't happen in the school—they happened before and after school, in many cases, on buses.

The district took a step back and thought about who was included in the district staff. They realized that a major and important part of their overall staff and operation was being eliminated from the training that worked so well in the classroom. The challenge to integrate all staff mem-bers—teachers, administrators, bus drivers, custodians, cooks, teacher's assistants—into the same program was be-fore them. A special in-service meeting was called, and the training was extended to the bus drivers.

The first year that drivers received training was quite eye-opening. Switching to a new discipline program in the middle of the school year did not lend itself to a smooth transition. Some of the bus drivers had been driving for more than 15 years and had their own way of taking care of problems. The district had a long-standing transportation policy on student behavior and subsequent penalties. When contacted for support, the school administrators were caught between programs. All of this had to be reviewed and adjusted so that implementation could actually happen and the district could operate with one program that would work for everyone. In short, RTP had to be used throughout the district, and that included on the school buses.

Our school district consists of six schools with approximately 3,000 students. Just over one third of the enrollment (1,100) use the school bus on a daily basis. There are 19 routes that service the different areas of the school district.

Our Process

The guiding principles of responsible thinking in a transportation setting dictate that the passengers have a right to safe transportation, and that the driver has a right to operate the bus safely, without distraction. These principles could have been posted on the bus and would have covered every situation that would arise. However, the drivers felt that, when dealing with younger students, easier-to-understand rules needed to be listed, instead. We use these eight rules:

1. Follow the driver's directions.
2. Stay in your seat and face forward.
3. Keep your hands and feet to yourself.
4. Put nothing out the window.
5. No refusing to share seat space.
6. No throwing of objects.
7. No degrading or abusive language or gestures.
8. No tobacco, drugs, or weapons of any kind.

When a new student comes into the district and begins to ride a bus, he is given a written overview of the transportation expectations, rules, and outcome possibilities. The form also requests information about grade, parental phone numbers, school, addresses, etc. The student returns the answered questions to the bus driver, who then adds the student to her rider list. The parent retains the transportation policy section for later reference.

A student may ride in any location on the bus that he chooses. If he chooses to break the rules, he also chooses the consequences that go with the rule. If a student has broken a rule and caused a hazardous situation on the bus, the driver will secure the bus and briefly work with the student. The driver will ask the same RTP questions used throughout the district. If the student refuses to follow the rules, or, if after having settled down, disrupts again, he has chosen to go to the front seat of the bus on the passenger side. The front seat on the bus serves as the RTC on the bus. The driver then fills out a multi-part Disciplinary Warning Form and sends it home with the student. The student must have a parent or guardian signature to get on the bus the following morning. The purpose of this form is to warn the appropriate people, including parents and school administrators, that the student is in danger of losing the privilege of riding the bus. While at school the next day, the student must obtain the signature of the RTC teacher. The student then returns the signed form to the bus driver before going home that day. Each person who signs the form retains one part of the form for their records—the parents have a copy, the school RTC teacher has a copy, and the driver has a copy. The final copy with all signatures replaces the driver copy.

The student is assigned to the front seat each time he rides the bus. Generally, it is recommended that the student ride in the front seat for at least one week, which gives the student sufficient time to demonstrate willingness to follow the rules. If all goes well, the student is allowed to move back a row for the next week. This process continues until the student has reached the area where he wants to sit. If things do not go well, the driver has the option of moving the student forward (either one seat or completely to the front) or extending the time that the student stays in the current position.

If the student who has been assigned to the front seat continues to make poor choices, he has chosen to leave the bus. The law in Idaho requires that if students are transported to school, they must also be transported home. The driver will complete a multi-part Loss of School Bus Privilege form and again send it with the student as he leaves the bus. This form specifically states that the parent or guardian is responsible for transporting the student to and from school. Principals have the option of extending this loss of school bus privilege to any of the field trips or other activities where buses are used.

The student takes the form home and has a parent sign the form and keep a copy. The parent then sees that the student gets to school the next morning. During the day, the student must go to the RTC teacher and get her signature on the form. The RTC teacher might also help direct the student in making a plan that will be acceptable to the school bus driver. After the student has completed the plan for returning to the bus, he takes it to the driver and negotiates with the driver for his return to the bus. The bus driver reviews the plan. If it is acceptable, the driver will sign the plan and give it back to the student. The student must return the plan to the RTC teacher, who will make copies and send them to the transportation office. The driver will also get a copy and can refer to it on the bus if the need arises. If the plan is not acceptable, the student may negotiate with the driver on what might be workable. As the student comes up with possible solutions, the driver or student can make notes or comments on the plan. Once everything is worked out, the driver sends the plan back to the RTC, and the student can rewrite the plan with the changes. The final version is sent to the driver for approval. Copies are then forwarded as necessary.

Our school district has a large number of field and activity trips during a school year. This necessitates sending route drivers on these trips and having substitute bus drivers take care of the local routes. There is the possibility that a substitute driver could come into contact with a student operating under an accepted plan. We concluded that if we had some record of what was happening on each bus route, we could give that information to the substitutes before they drove. This would provide consistency for both drivers and students.

We found that an unused time card rack was the answer. Each route was given a slot with its number on it. If a student were assigned a seat, the driver would create a "time card" for the student. It would contain the student's name, grade, school, and bus number. The driver would then use each day on the card as a status indicator. If the student was assigned to a front seat, the seat assignment and the date that it became effective would be listed. When a student was moved, the card would be updated. All of the cards for each bus go into the same slot in the card rack. A substitute driver can get the entire stack of cards, review them, and thus be current on what has been happening on the bus.

Success Rates

After we started using this program in the fall of 1996, we began tracking the number of discipline occurrences. We researched the previous two years under our old program and compared end-of-year results from the first year of the RTP program.

Year:	1994–95	1995–96	1996–97
Number of student discipline problems:	171	178	108

The results show a drop of about 40% in the number of discipline referrals or warnings that were issued the first year with RTP. We are currently in the second year. This year, Ed returned and helped us deal with some questions. After the completion of that in-service, we are more focused in the direction in which we are progressing.

In closing, a couple of amusing anecdotes:

Just after beginning to use this program, a driver was faced with a safety hazard situation on the bus. She started by asking a student, "What are you doing?" The student stopped, paused, looked at her and simply replied, "Are you guys doing that too?"

An eighth grade student had chosen the front seat. He rode the bus in that seat home, and the following day he confirmed with the driver that he was now in the second seat. The driver informed him that each seat assignment was for a week, not a day. She told him that if he misbehaved, he would move forward, instead of backward. The student was shocked. In his most frustrated voice, he said that he would end up in the front seat until he graduated from high school! As they were on the way home, he told the driver that he wouldn't ride the bus again. He was going to ride with his sister, instead. For a few weeks, the student wasn't seen on the bus. Then he started riding again, and he appropriately took his assigned seat. The driver asked him about riding with his sister. He just looked out the window and said that she wouldn't let him ride with her either!

I know that my day is easier because of RTP. I spend less time on student discipline problems and can focus on the rest of my responsibilities.

RESPONSIBLE THINKING PROCESS
FOR SCHOOL BUS DRIVERS

A safe and effective approach to student discipline
by Edward E. Ford - based on perceptual control theory
from his book - Discipline for Home and School

*For children to succeed, they must believe you care about them and
that you have confidence in their ability to find solutions to their
problems. The stronger the relationship, the easier it is to resolve the
differences between you. If done in a respectful manner, this
responsible thinking process can help build that relationship. It also
teaches self-discipline through responsible thinking. Ask questions in
a calm, respectful, curious voice. Never yell or tell, always ask. Avoid
excuses by not asking WHY.*

- WHAT ARE YOU DOING?

WHAT ARE THE RULES ON THIS BUS?

WHAT HAPPENS WHEN YOU BREAK THE RULES?

IS THAT WHAT YOU WANT TO HAPPEN?

WHERE DO YOU WANT TO SIT, HERE OR THE FRONT
SEAT?

- WHAT WILL HAPPEN THE NEXT TIME YOU
CREATE A SAFETY HAZARD OR BREAK THE RULES?

WHEN CHILD AVOIDS DEALING WITH YOU

If they avoid answering a question, repeat it. If they persist in not dealing
with you, then ask . . .

DO YOU WANT TO STAY WHERE YOU ARE OR MOVE
TO THE FRONT OF THE BUS?

If they continue to avoid dealing with you, or, if after settling down, they
again begin to distract you, it means they don't want to follow the rules
and have chosen to go to the front of the bus. Then say . . .

I SEE YOU HAVE CHOSEN THE FRONT SEAT.

Once you have said this, never back down. The child must move at
once to the front seat. He should be issued a citation for refusing to follow
bus rules and the principal and parents notified that he has created a
safety hazard by distracting the driver, thus endangering the lives of the
students. At the next safety violation, the child has, by his actions, chosen
not to ride the bus. Obviously, the ability to implement this process will
depend on school district policy and state laws.

(continued on back)

CREATING A PLAN

The following might help in creating a form for use in making a specific plan: Have the child write down (1) what she/he did, (2) what rule was violated, and (3) how she/he is going to deal with the same problem in the future. The child should first try her/his plan in the front seat. Then, at the discretion of the driver, the child moves toward her/his regular seat (see "Use of Front Seat" paragraph below). The student and driver should sign and date the form.

WHEN THE CHILD RETURNS TO THE BUS

Upon returning to the bus, the child must negotiate his plan with the driver. This process of negotiating with the driver can help to build in children respect for the driver's authority. Working out a plan also teaches children to organize their thinking and to search for ways to create plans that will help them respect school bus safety. The following questions should help you evaluate how you are teaching this process:
1. Do you always give the child adequate time to discuss her/his plan?
2. Do you suggest alternatives when the plan is unacceptable?
3. Does your child perceive you as wanting her/him to succeed?
4. When you tell a child anything, who is doing the thinking? When you ask, who is doing the thinking? Are you teaching the child to think?

USE OF FRONT SEAT AND RETURN TO REGULAR SEAT

Whether the child has chosen to leave the bus and is now returning or has chosen the front seat after breaking a rule, she/he must demonstrate safe, responsible behavior in the front seat before being allowed to move to other seats. Regardless of whether it is a first-time offense or not, it is strongly recommended that the child be moved one or two seats at a time. This gradual return to her/his regularly assigned seat allows time for the child to rebuild confidence in her/his own ability to demonstrate bus safety and respect for others.

SUGGESTED BUS RULES

YOU CANNOT VIOLATE THE RIGHTS OF THOSE ON THE BUS
The bus driver has a right to drive safely without being distracted
Children have a right to ride in safety
Some specific rules:
• stay in seat and face forward
• hands and feet to yourself
• nothing out the window
• no abusive language
• no throwing anything • no refusing to share seat with another
• no degrading or improper language or gestures

Brandt Publishing / Ed Ford & Associates
10209 N. 56th St., Scottsdale, Arizona 85253 Ph. 602-991-4860

Visit Our Web Page - http://www.respthink.com/

Chapter 27
RTP in a Residential School Setting on a Navajo Reservation

Rod Bond
Lead Teacher
Lukachukai Community School
Lukachukai, Arizona

Lukachukai Community School is a Bureau of Indian Affairs K–8 school on the Navajo Reservation in northern Arizona. It is a boarding school with an enrollment of approximately 400 students, a fourth of whom board at the school Monday through Thursday in a dormitory. The school is located remotely, with Gallup, New Mexico, the nearest city.

Many of the students live in even more remote areas, with very poor roads; some have homes with no electricity or running water, and some live in hogans with dirt floors. Many do not live with their natural parents, but with grandparents or other relatives.

The Navajo Nation, with an unemployment rate of 47%, has many families below the U.S. poverty level. Alcoholism and physical and sexual abuse are prevalent, with more than 90% of our students being affected in some way by these problems. The Navajos are struggling between two worlds, that of their traditions, which they are trying to maintain, and that of the dominant society. The students, most of whom speak both Navajo and English, often do not have a very high level of comprehension of English.

But in many ways, the students are no different from students elsewhere in the U.S. They can become institutionalized, as has occurred in the past, either "going along to get along" or "rebelling" against the setting in which they find themselves. Their other alternative—and this fits closely with the Navajo traditions—is to develop a sense of self-confidence in themselves and respect for others. And this is the heart of RTP: the students learn to think and to deal with their problems in a responsible way, especially after they have learned to make effective plans.

The residential setting provides some extra and unique opportunities for implementing the responsible thinking process. In this situation, it can become a process that touches each and every part of a student's life, five days a week, 24 hours a day. For this to take place, however, the residential staff has to be perceived not just as "people who have been hired to watch the kids and make sure they don't get into trouble." Rather, they must be an integral part of the overall responsible thinking process, as well as capable of helping the students to develop their skills in the basic academic courses, such as reading, writing, and math. Because of recent developments, they should also be computer literate. The residential staff needs the same RTP training as the academic staff, faculty, and administrators of the school.

At our school, many students arrive without the necessary skills of time management, and the constant complaint from teachers regarding the lack of homework has shown that the students desperately need to learn the discipline of study. This involves the ability to set aside some specific time each night, avoiding distractions that are normal in a dormitory setting, devoting this time to academic work. Even those students without any homework should learn to use this time for educational purposes, such as reading, typing, or developing computer skills.

With a qualified dorm staff capable of creating the proper setting so that students can have the opportunity to learn the discipline of study, this can easily be achieved. The staff should set aside specific times for study throughout the dorm, eliminating distractions such as television and interactive games, so that all students have a place to study without being disturbed. Those students who want to work together on a project, or for a test, can work out a pre-arranged agreement with the dorm staff so that this process won't interfere with other students who require a quiet atmosphere. As I mentioned above, those students who have no assigned homework should still have to fill this study time with some type of academic work.

As students begin to understand the importance of study time and want more time to finish their homework, certain locations in the dorm should be created for such needs. As students acquire the self-confidence that comes with the success of completing homework and academic projects, their self-esteem begins to build, and they begin to exhibit good citizenship and community service.

These ideas can be expanded and built upon through a "mentor" program. This could begin first with the boarding students and eventually evolve to the entire student body. Each student would be asked to write down, in order of preference, those adults with whom he would like to deal—those to whom he could go for help with various problems. Beginning with the oldest students, the adults would be assigned to those students who wanted them as mentors. This way, older students would be more likely to get their first preferences. The reason for having students pick the persons with whom they want to work is that they would be the persons with whom the student would be most inclined to work with, to deal with. The mentors, in turn, would have the advantage of having students that wanted them, that saw them as persons who could be of help.

A mentor should be sent copies of the student's grade records. The teachers now would have someone whom they could contact if the student fell behind in his work, or if the student had behavioral difficulties in school or else-where on the school campus. Also, the RTC teacher and administrators would have an automatic member of an intervention team if such were required for the student. And the parents now would have someone to see when they had concerns about their child.

This mentor program can be expanded to the entire staff of the school, and the student's choice can be from administrators, teachers, coaches, and other appropriate personnel. The more options there are, the fewer students each of the adults will have, thus allowing for more personal time with each student. This mentor program should naturally evolve to a sense of community within the dormitory, the classroom, the total school, and, ultimately, the community. This would be especially true in remote areas, where the school is often the focal point of activities and leadership. This involves not only parents, but everyone in the community, and it could be accomplished with the students leading the way.

The discipline of study program and, especially, the mentor program can have far reaching effects. Instead of students being a problem, they could very well become part of the solution. They could be a hope for the future.

Chapter 28
The Coach's Corner

Bill McCarrick
Head Football Coach and RTC Teacher
Morrice High School
Morrice, Michigan

My coaching background is probably very similar to most. I started coaching 23 years ago with youth league football and baseball teams. I moved up to junior high and then into high school, and I have spent the last four years as head football coach here at Morrice. My first year here, we were 2-7, and my second year, we were 3-6. The school had only one winning season in the previous 12 years, but I was sure we could turn this program around, because we had great kids. The problem was convincing them that they could win.

My first step was to get on staff. I felt it was important to be in the same building with the kids I was coaching. The job I applied for was a new position opening for the next year, a position in the school's new RTC. Great, I thought, I'm the perfect choice. I could picture myself as the tough football coach carrying a big stick. Boy, I thought, I would be great at this job!

Joe Sierzenga, principal of our elementary school, was in charge of the interviews. Again I thought, great, I've known Joe for a long time, and, in fact, he was responsible for me getting the coaching job at Morrice. Joe told me at a pre-interview that I needed to read the book he handed me, *Discipline for Home and School*. I read it quickly, and I thought it had some great ideas that I could incorporate into my way of thinking. I was thankful he gave it to me. The time for the interview came, and I walked in very confidently and sat in front of a panel of three people, one of course being Joe. I really hadn't prepared for the interview, expecting the usual questions that answer themselves and thinking that all they would require of me would be to put a positive slant on what they wanted to hear. I soon found out this was different—much different. I had to think and answer questions about ideas from Ed Ford's book. My mind-set going in was that the book was a guideline for the RTC. I had no idea that the book was the *exact* guideline for that room, and I didn't realize the change in attitude that it would require from me.

That interview changed my life. It was the beginning of a new mind-set that not only enabled me to run the RTC, but also drastically changed how I coach football. After understanding and applying the principles of RTP, our team went 9-3. It was the first team in school history to make the state play-offs, and one of only two teams in the history of our county to become regional champions. Our loss in the state semifinal was to the eventual state champions. Last year, we graduated 10 of our total 18 players, accounting for 16 out of 22 starting spots. This year, we took second in the conference but made the state play-offs, and, like last year, our loss was to the eventual state champions. The difference is unquestionably the use of RTP and a good solid understanding of PCT, plus the permanent mind-set it has created in me and our coaching staff. Understanding PCT allows us to apply RTP a lot better.

By nature, football coaches are control freaks. We want to control *everything*: what our players eat, the time they go to bed, and even what they should be thinking about on game day. After my interview with Joe, I started asking myself why I do certain things. I wanted absolutely no talking on the bus to away games. Why? "No, you can't play that noise you call music in the locker room." Why? "You guys are going to work your butts off to win a championship." Why? "I don't care if you like me, but you *are* going to respect me." Why? "This is *my* team and you are going to act and perform the way I want you to." Why? "My coach

treated me like this so I'm going to treat you the same."
Why? After I understood the concepts of control and
counter-control, we had a team meeting. In that meeting, I
learned that "my" players wanted pretty much the same
thing I wanted. I learned that "my" players knew that the
way to achieve the things we wanted was pretty much how
I knew we must achieve them. I discovered that "my" players hated it when team members missed practice as much
as I did, and for the same reasons. But mostly I discovered
that they were not "my" players—that each member was a
part of our team, and that I was only a part of the team as
well. I discovered that we each have responsibilities, and
that we all must trust each other to carry out those responsibilities. I discovered that all of the yelling and screaming
didn't help them at all—that it was impossible to truly communicate with them, because they were afraid of me and
afraid of making mistakes. When I got all the right answers
in practice, I became so frustrated when they did the wrong
things in a game. I discovered that was because they gave
me the right answers even though they didn't understand
the answers or how to apply them in a game. The respect I
thought I had by mentally and emotionally beating them
into shape (submission) was my fear of not being good
enough to earn their respect.

Now, we have many team meetings, and I ask a lot of
questions. I never tell them what to do; I ask them, and I
encourage them to make good choices. The decision to
practice longer is their choice, because they know we need
more work. A great example of this happened just two
weeks ago. We had five Junior Varsity players ineligible, and
two Varsity players who were close. The decision was made
to have them run five time laps, which are timed 225-yard
sprints. At the end of practice, right after we ran a 10-
minute interval run, I called the violators to the field and
lined them up, ready to run. I noticed a player there who
wasn't on the list. I asked him what he was doing here, and
he said to me, "Coach, I'm doing these, too. These are my
team mates, and we do things together." He ran all five

killer sprints, encouraging his team mates all the way, and afterwards he offered to help them in their classes.

Another time, five players were late for practice. We decided that they would do extra time laps. The whole team did theirs, and I asked the violators to step up. The entire team was there and did the extra laps. Now, in the old days, I might have been tempted to make the whole team run the extra laps to create peer pressure to do the right things. Having the team volunteer to act like a team was extremely satisfying.

Once last year, a Tuesday practice was running long. It hadn't been a great practice, and after practice, the players had to set up tables for a fund-raising dinner. I looked at my watch, decided I should dismiss them, and pulled them together to do our practice-ending breakdown. But before I could dismiss them, they asked me if I was forgetting something. I thought and said, "No, I don't think so." They reminded me that it was Tuesday, and on Tuesdays we always do hard calls—practice isn't over until that happens. So, of course, we did hard calls. In fact, it was the hardest session of the season. They collectively knew what it took to win, and they didn't want to leave any stone unturned.

Toward the end of last season, we had a player with "girlfriend problems" who skipped practice without letting me know about his special situation. Our attendance policy was that any player with two unexcused practices was off the team, and this was his second. The player was not a very popular kid. Our captains approached me and voiced their concern about losing one of our 18 players: "What would happen if we got into a situation where we needed him?" I asked them, "What do you want to have happen?" They asked if they could meet with him and asked if they could include all the seniors. The next day after school, at the meeting, they asked the player why he missed practice. He explained his problems with his girlfriend and apologized for missing practice. The team members all asked very pertinent questions. They talked about the team goals they had set. The seniors talked about his importance to the team.

They asked him if he wanted to be on the team. "Do you want to do your part?" The young man, in tears, said this to the team: "I never realized until this moment how much this team and you guys mean to me." He continued, "I understand the rules. I'm not blaming anyone for being off the team, but if you let me back on, I'll never let you down again." All of the players went to him and shook his hand, turned to me, and said, "If we could, we would like to see him back on the team. We are sure he'll do his part from now on." I simply said, "If that's what you want, it's fine with me." I could have been mad or worried that they were undermining the rules that had been set. I had previously thought that the meeting might get messy with anger, denials, and accusations. I thought I would have to referee it. But I never said a word. The things they were discussing didn't really pertain to me. I was very happy and very proud of these young men who put aside the stuff that was unimportant and made a decision based on the goals they had collectively set. I realized again that this wasn't "my" team, that I was only a *part* of it. I've never been more proud of a team. The team belonged to them.

Before they hired me at Morrice, I spent many seasons on the sidelines as an assistant coach at another school. In those years, I remember many, many kids coming off the field after being yelled at by the coach, and, as soon as the coach left the area, they called the coach names and said very disrespectful things. The response from the coach? "He got mad—he'll get over it. No big deal." My assistant coaches tell me that in the last two years not one of our players has said anything disrespectful toward me at any time.

With this new mind-set and different approach, it might seem that I don't need to yell. Wrong. I yell as much now as I ever have. The difference is that the players understand my role, which is to challenge them to get better, to show some intensity, and to be a leader. When I do yell, the things I yell are said in a positive way. I never feel a need to tear down a player or to yell at a player because his performance has made me mad. I trust them to be giving us a great effort.

There is no fear in them that if they screw up, the coach is going to kill them or (even worse) bench them. We preach that there are about 150 plays in a game, and it's the next one that we have to get right. It doesn't matter how bad or how well we did on the last one. Get ready for the next one. I never yell about something that happened on the last play, but I use that information to help them do it right on the next play.

I still have an urge to control things, but I force myself to think it through and let the kids decide. I would like them to wear white socks at home. They wear black. I would like the locker room to be absolutely quiet. They have blaring noise that they call music. I would like them to be absolutely quiet on the bus on the way to games. They usually are, because they understand how visualization works and how it is important to be mentally and emotionally ready to play. When they are not quiet, a red warning flag goes up that they might not be emotionally ready to play. If I required them to be quiet, would I know that? Now I'm better able to see their emotional state and possibly prevent an unmotivated performance. I allow our football players to play in the school band during pre-game and at half-time. Do I like it? No. But I trust them to get the information they need to be ready to play, and they always do.

So, though it seems a little strange to me, I stop worrying about the little things. I'm able to concentrate on what I need to do, and I'm sure I do a much better job of it. If you give them responsibility, you are also giving them ownership in the team, and if the team is theirs, they are going to work a lot harder and execute things much better. We all pay lip service to the fact that this is "our" team, but how many coaches are willing to give control to all members of the team?

Now, let's stop and step back and look at the bigger picture. This year, I have two young men playing football who nobody would have believed could be staying on the team. Both young men were very "frequent fliers" in the RTC the year before. Derick was expelled from a school in another state for bringing a weapon to school. The other boy had been in a great deal of gang-related trouble in a previous school. By my working with these two young men in the RTC and treating them with respect, they got a little better. I began to genuinely like them and really cared about them. I would go to bat for them, making sure they were given a fair deal when they messed up. We started to make goals that began to seem possible for them. They both watched football players come into the room and saw how they acted and how they were treated. After a while, both young men asked about playing football. Lonny, one of the young men, had missed a lot of class time and had to stay many hours during the summer to make up time to get the credits he needed to play. He did this without my involvement. He wanted to play. He wanted his life to go in a different direction. He made up the time, was able to play, and has done a great job. The teachers are amazed at the turn-around. Lonny loves the person he has become. The self-esteem that he created has launched him into a future that has real hope. I am very, very proud of him, and I tell him that often. The way he smiles shows that he appreciates the fact that someone believes in him.

The second young man, after getting into a fight in the RTC, scared me. I really thought this kid was trouble. I was afraid that he would seriously hurt somebody. He so convinced me of this that I told our principal that we should not allow him to be here. As time went by, he began to get in less trouble, other students didn't pick on him as much, and he began to laugh and smile more, until one day he asked, "What would you think if I signed up for football?" I really didn't think it would ever happen. I was sure that the first time he was told to do something he didn't like, he would quit. But of course, I said something like, "I think football would be great for you." When August came around, he was there. I thought, "Good for him." A week later, when he was still out, I stopped to think about what football offered him. We have since become friends. One of our team rules is that no one is allowed to say anything negative about another team member, so he must have felt safe. He was very proud that he didn't quit, as I'm sure he probably thought that he would.

Football is a great vehicle for teaching responsibility. The players can witness in the short term the life-long benefits of RTP training. I know it makes my job a heck of a lot easier. I can, for the first time, trust my players to do what is expected of them—because the expectations are theirs, not mine. And, oh, what a difference!

Chapter 29
A Janitor Sees All

Bryan John Williams
Janitor-Groundsman
Morningside State School
Brisbane, Queensland, Australia

I first met Bryan in the school yard. He had been work-ing at the school for 10 years, had two children who had graduated from the school, and a son, B. J., in seventh grade. When he first noticed that the "kids had changed," he was unaware that RTP was being used. When he told the principal of the changes he'd seen, she invited him to write about what he'd seen and to take part in the RTP training. Here is what he wrote.

—*Ed Ford*

I have found that since RTP began in our school a num-ber of things have changed. The behavior of the children is an example of the changes. There are now no cheeky kids around. No basketballs on the walkways. No more smart alec remarks. Children like to help with rubbish. They like to help clean the school yard and gardens. It's a pleasure to walk around the school yard and see how the atmosphere in this school has changed. The kids seem a lot happier now, not so much fighting and arguing. The children keep the toilets cleaner. They treat one another with more re-spect and play better together. I think this works on teach-ers as well, as I don't hear them yelling any more.

Chapter 30
How I Became an RTP Trainer

Tim Carey
Advisory Visiting Teacher
Brisbane, Queensland, Australia

As interest in Ed Ford's RTP program grows in Australia, a number of people have asked me how they might go about becoming trainers. The process of becoming a trainer in Ed's organization is very different from the process that exists in other organizations. Whereas in some organizations to become a trainer you just have to attend a number of training workshops and complete a set amount of courses, to become a trainer in RTP you have to demonstrate that you are able to successfully assist people in educational settings to implement this process. Assisting people to implement RTP might sound simple, but my experience has been that this is something that takes a great deal of time, persistence, and learning. In fact, learning is perhaps the key. Paradoxically, my intention when I first discovered Ed's program was not to become a trainer. Instead my intention was, and still is, to learn as much as possible about RTP and PCT. If learning RTP and PCT is your goal, and you spend a great deal of time at this, then becoming a trainer will look after itself.

For several years, I have worked as a behavior management specialist with the education department in Queensland, Australia. Although I have a teaching background, I have also done formal studies in psychology, and I have completed many informal courses and workshops on various counseling and behavior management approaches. From my very early days of teaching, I have been interested in why we do the things we do as human beings. I have been interested in the answer to this problem, not at a specific level of why a certain person does a particular thing, but at the general level of why human beings do anything at all. To my way of thinking, part of the answer to this problem must include an explanation of the way we might be put together that allows us to act on the world.

While the answer to this query seems to me to be of paramount significance, it led me for many years to a great deal of disillusionment and frustration. What I was looking for was a theory of behavior that would explain all human behavior. My experience, however, was that all of the training I undertook consisted of an ever-increasing array of nifty strategies that you could try in different situations. Some courses talk about having a theory underpinning their nifty strategies, but to me, the explanations they propose for human behavior are superficial in the extreme. A minute or two's introspection soon reveals that such theories cannot possibly account for the subjective experiences we have that we know as behavior.

Try it yourself: Is there anything in the environment that makes you do the things you do? What if you decide you don't want that particular thing any more? Or what if you discover that the particular thing you like is only being made available to you so that you will act in certain ways that another person wants to see? Can this thing still make you do things? If not, then a theory proposing that environmental effects control behavior has some serious problems.

What about an explanation suggesting that we make plans in our heads and then carry them out? Try that. Make a plan tonight for how much you need to turn the hot and cold taps to make the water temperature in the shower comfortable, carry out the plan, and then step in. To me, a theory that doesn't account for someone doing the wash—and hence reducing the temperature of the hot water—at the same time that you are taking a shower has some problems.

Finally, is a theory that says we have a number of needs

that must be met able to explain behavior? Even if we consider a fairly basic need like the need for food and water, how does this explanation account for the behavior of hunger strikers, anorexics, and fast food junkies? Obviously, this theory cannot.

Pursuit of a robust explanation of human behavior did not make me popular with many of my colleagues, either. Many times I would find myself in discussions about why a child was doing a particular thing and what should be done about it. While I believe that everyone involved in the discussions had good intentions about helping children, many of the approaches I saw had some initial early success, only to fail later on. More and more, it seemed to me that it was the child, not the expert, who was deciding whether or not a particular intervention would be a success. There was no theory I could find that could account for the behavior of every human being in every situation. I found this troubling in the extreme. I was troubled partly because I consider it unethical to work with other human beings without an adequate explanation of human behavior underpinning everything I do, and I was also troubled because many of my colleagues didn't understand what a theory is.

And then it happened. I was introduced to perceptual control theory. There seemed to be something different about this theory, and I began to search for information about it. I started to scour the Internet, and I found the Control Systems Group. I knew as soon as I started to read information about PCT that I had found what I was looking for. In fact, PCT was *more* than I was looking for. PCT does not just explain the behavior of human beings, it explains the behavior of all living things. Even more important for me, as I reflected on my own experiences, I realized that this theory explained my behavior *from my perspective*. As I read through the CSG net site, I discovered that there was a man by the name of Ed Ford, who was working on building a discipline program in schools that was based on the principles of PCT. I knew immediately that the focus of my work would change forever.

My first step was to purchase copies of Ed's books. I read these and became incredibly excited at the possibilities of his program. I obtained Ed's telephone number from the back of the book and phoned him. As we spoke, I became more and more convinced that this program would make a significant and important contribution to all areas of education. This conviction has never wavered, and has instead grown. During that first telephone conversation, I learned about Tom Bourbon, who was conducting scientific research on Ed's program. I made a later phone call to Ed when Tom was with him, and the three of us spoke about the program. At the end of the conversation, we exchanged e-mail addresses, but I don't think any of us guessed where this would lead.

I realized very early on in my learning of RTP that it was PCT that made this program successful. If the strategies advocated by Ed were used by someone who subscribed to an alternative explanation of behavior, the program would be compromised. Understanding and adhering to PCT principles is crucial for the program to be effective. I began then to exchange e-mail messages with Tom, learning all I could about PCT. My understanding is still not where I would like it to be; however, it has grown enormously since I first began the exchanges with Tom.

RTP is not a "recipe" for success in schools. Ed would never be able to anticipate every problem that every school might encounter and design a program to solve these problems. Instead, Ed suggests a *process* that can be learned and adapted to suit different situations. In fact, that's why Ed says that all of us can participate in RTP's growth and development. It is important that the process be learned well, however, because while the implementation of the process will differ from situation to situation, its core aspects will remain the same. In order to learn the process well, an understanding of PCT is essential.

Whenever a problem is encountered with RTP, it is to the principles of PCT that I turn for guidance. I know that if what I am doing is consistent with PCT, then my practices will remain closely aligned to RTP.

Over time, I have noticed my understanding changing in significant ways. I no longer think of people reacting in situations. I have become less interested in the actions that I see, and more interested in what might be going on for the people from their own perspectives. I also have begun to appreciate how different the "real" world is for each of us, and the dangers of making assumptions about how others think about particular issues. And I have become aware that the labels we apply to children are irrelevant. More and more, I am realizing that when we see children behave, what we are seeing is a by-product of their attempt to experience the world in the way they want to experience it. I now understand the problems I encounter in schools as problems of control, and I recognize how conflicts can arise when control systems share the same environment.

As my understanding of PCT developed, I became increasingly concerned about my ability to make links between PCT and RTP. As well as communicating with Tom, therefore, I began to include Ed in our e-mail conversations. After working in schools with students and teachers, I would send a list of questions to Ed and Tom. They both were incredible in their responsiveness. Time after time, I received lengthy answers to my questions, which I would spend hours reading and attempting to understand. Often, the replies that Ed and Tom sent would generate more questions from me, and again I would receive detailed replies. My lessons, therefore, were determined entirely by me and were centered around what I needed to know. This was very different from other training programs in which I had participated, where the content was predetermined, and small groups of people would all receive the same information. Many times, Ed and Tom would answer my questions with their own questions. Again, this was a different teaching approach than others I had encountered, but it meant that I was an active participant in the process. I didn't merely sit there and just receive information;

instead, I had to do a great deal of thinking and seeking out of answers on my own. This approach was frustrating and time-consuming, but infinitely more rewarding in the long run. I now have the resources to find many of the answers to my own questions.

Along with the e-mail conversations, I spent a great deal of time reading all of the PCT material I could find and experiencing computer demonstrations of PCT ideas. I have never tired of learning about this theory, and I find that I still get new information every time I see Ed and Tom give workshops. I still find myself discovering new insights and implications of the theory, and experiencing "Aha" moments with PCT. One of the important aspects of Ed's approach that is different from other approaches is that Ed promotes a process, not a program. The implication for me is that this is not something that I can just learn and then go and do. This is an approach that requires continual revisiting.

My understanding of PCT has helped me enormously when I am using Ed's process in my work with young people. When I am helping young people, if at any time I am stuck and have trouble deciding what to do, I am able to return to the principles of PCT. Being able to appreciate that the person in front of me is a living control system who is simply trying to experience the world as he or she would prefer it to be has helped me enormously. I have found that using the process Ed teaches is an incredibly uplifting experience for both me and the young people I work with. I cannot describe the thrill I experience of seeing young people learning to control their perceptions in a way that assists them to operate more successfully as human beings. The looks on their faces as they begin to work at plans and achieve their goals are intensely rewarding to me.

My journey as a trainer is not complete. Although I am honored to have received this recognition from Ed, I realize that I will never stop learning, and that in order to grow in knowledge of PCT and RTP, I *cannot* stop learning. I need to work hard, for example, at using this process with adults. Adults, too, seem to function more effectively when they are asked questions rather than being told; however, I find this difficult to do. I continue to work at learning the theory and the process, and I find my confidence and effectiveness grows accordingly.

I believe that RTP is possibly the most significant contribution that has been made to education since schools were invented. This process impacts on all facets of people's lives and enables them to live in harmony within themselves, and peacefully and successfully with other people. Even when this process is not done well in schools, it still seems to be more effective than the myriad of other behavior management approaches. When it is done well, it has a beauty and an elegance that have profound effects—so profound, in fact, that I believe we do not yet fully appreciate how powerful this approach really is. I look forward to the future, when we are able to investigate how children who participated in RTP are living their lives as adults, and how their children function when they arrive at school. Potentially, I believe that RTP, with PCT as a backing, has the ability to change society. For now, RTP is a nice place to start.

Chapter 31
Perceptual Control Theory in the Classroom

W. Thomas Bourbon
Perceptual Control Theorist
Houston, Texas

In Chapter 2, Ed briefly introduces some principles of perceptual control theory (PCT), the theory he relied on when he designed his responsible thinking process (RTP). In that chapter, he describes events occurring when Hunter tries to attract the attention of Sally Ann, and when Mrs. Johnson intervenes to maintain a quiet classroom. In this chapter, I introduce additional concepts from PCT and illustrate them with more interactions among Hunter, Sally Ann, and Mrs. Johnson. I hope that this additional introduction gives you a sampling of the rigor and depth of PCT: it is different from all other theories in behavioral science, social science, and life science.

Reviewing the basics: PCT explains how each of us controls (specifies, creates, and maintains) some of our own perceptions, in spite of the fact that, in the world around us, natural forces and other people can always disturb the perceptions that we control. Stop reading for a while and become aware of your perceptions of your surroundings, and of your own body. Become aware of what you see, hear, smell, taste, and feel. Now make some of those perceptions change. (Act so as to change what you see, hear, feel, and so on.) Become aware of any perceptions that change independently of what you do. (Do you see, hear, or feel anything changing, independently of what you do?) Think back to Chapter 2 and identify examples of Hunter acting to create perceptions for himself, and of Mrs. Johnson experiencing changes in her perceptions, changes that occurred independently of what she was doing at the time.

In PCT, the experiences you just had are what we mean by the word "perception." All of our experiences of the world, including experiences of our own bodies and actions, are perceptions. Perceptions can range from those of the presence and intensity of sounds or lights, through those of the fact that a person is standing in front of us or that a particular tune is playing on the radio, to those about the state of the world economy and the quality of our relationships with other people. PCT explains behavioral actions as the means by which a person affects the world in order to create and maintain certain perceptions. We always act to make what we perceive happening right now match what we intend to perceive right now. For so long as what we perceive to be happening matches what we intend to perceive, we do not change what we are doing; when there is a mismatch between perceptions right now and our intended perceptions, we change the way we act on the world in order to change what we perceive. The mismatch between intended perceptions and actual ones is what drives any changes in our actions. Just like Hunter when he counteracted Mrs. Johnson's attempt to stop his communication with Sally Ann, we act to counteract, or eliminate, the effects of anything in the world that disturbs our controlled perceptions. For us to control a given perception, our actions must vary any way necessary to eliminate the effects of disturbances.

We control (specify, create, and maintain) our perceptions, not our actions. We are aware of the perceptions we control (the position of our car on the highway, the temperature of the room, the degree to which our dinner is seasoned), but we are often blissfully unaware of our specific actions by which we control those perceptions. If anyone asks us what we are doing, most of us describe the perception we are controlling (driving my car to the hospital in an emergency; working hard to complete a project, in a room that feels too hot; eating this dinner prepared by my spouse, a dinner which, by the way, is too bland), not our actions at the moment. On the other hand, all that another person can see are the actions we use to control our perceptions; the other person cannot experience our perceptions and often believes that we are "doing" our actions (gripping the steering wheel and turning it, manipulating the controls on a thermostat, shaking a pepper shaker above a serving tray).

Think back to Chapter 2. What would Mrs. Johnson perceive Hunter doing? What would Hunter say he is doing? What would Hunter perceive Mrs. Johnson doing? What would she say she is doing? What would Sally Ann say she is doing? If you understand the differences between the perceptions Hunter, Sally Ann, and Mrs. Johnson control (what each of them would say he or she is doing), and what each of them perceives the other doing, then you are in a good position to understand PCT. If you understand PCT, you have a better chance of recognizing its importance as a source of new ideas about how people can interact.

A little beyond the basics—disturbing one another: Of all the perceptions that a person experiences at any moment, he selects only a few to control. As far as he is concerned, all of the others go uncontrolled. When Hunter decided to control his perceptions of Sally Ann, he gave up control over many of his other perceptions, like the ones related to completing his spelling exercise and to minding the rules in the classroom. Also, his actions had many more effects than just the ones he intended. For example, the second time Hunter acted to control his perceptions of Sally Ann, Mrs. Johnson (and probably other students) also heard the sounds he made. All that Hunter intended was to perceive Sally Ann change what she was doing. He probably did not intend to disturb other students, and he certainly did not intend for Mrs. Johnson to hear him, or warn him. We are all like Hunter, in that our actions always produce many more consequences than the ones we intend. We often do not even perceive those unintended consequences of our own actions, but sometimes they disturb perceptions other people control. Unintentionally, Hunter's signals to Sally Ann disturbed Mrs. Johnson's controlled perception of "a quiet classroom." Even if we do not intend for our actions to disturb other people, from time to time they will.

Disturbances that occur in a classroom are often called "disruptions," and the person who disrupts is often disciplined. Usually, an educator intends for discipline to "make" a student stop performing actions that occur during a disruption—actions that disturb perceptions the educator controls. This is where the ideas in PCT become important. Discipline is the means by which educators are supposed to control the actions of students, but we know that people, including students, do not "do" their actions. Instead, actions are the means by which people control their perceptions. In that light, we see that discipline is the means by which educators try to control their own perceptions of what happens in the classroom.

We also know that disturbances to others often occur as unintended consequences when a person acts to control her perceptions. If we try to stop her from performing those actions, then she might very well oppose the effects of our efforts, which act as disturbances to her controlled perceptions. Her opposition is part of the perfectly natural attempt to eliminate the effects of disturbances, and it is not necessarily a sign that she is nasty, defiant, or oppositional. The student might not have realized that her actions disturbed perceptions controlled by other students or by the teacher, and the teacher might not have known that his disciplinary actions would be opposed as disturbances to perceptions the student controlled.

It looks like we have entered into a potentially endless knot of social complexity, produced when each of us disturbs the other's perceptions and then attempts to eliminate the effects of those disturbances. The only way to cut that knot is for us to acknowledge that all of us act to control our own perceptions, and that sometimes we disturb

one another. Then we must develop ways to eliminate unnecessary disturbances to others, and to resolve conflicts
that often ensue when unavoidable disturbances occur.

Feedback functions: Look back at the diagrams in Chapter 2 that represent Hunter as a perceptual control system. Notice the arrow that connects Hunter's "actions" to
the "controlled variable." Scientific PCT includes a formal
mathematical model of a control system and how it inter-
acts with its environment. In the model, the arrow that connects actions to controlled variables is called the "feedback
function," the physical pathway that joins the person's actions to the things in the world that affect his controlled
perceptions. Some feedback functions are simple and direct, others are extremely long and complex. If Hunter begins to lose interest in his spelling lesson and decides to tap
his fingers on the desk, the feedback function is short and
direct: his motor neurons act on the muscles in his fingers,
and the muscles pull against the bones in his fingers, which
immediately move to produce tapping. Hunter quickly and
reliably produces the perceptions he intends. Of course,
his tapping might disturb someone else—like Mrs. Johnson.

If Hunter wants to sharpen his pencil, the feedback function is a little more complex than the one for tapping. Now
Hunter's actions result in the pencil being inside the sharpener and the handle of the sharpener turning. Turning the
handle causes a series of mechanical events, inside the
sharpener, that result in the pencil being sharpened. In this
case, the feedback function includes a few mechanical objects and events in the environment outside of Hunter's
body. (For a moment, imagine that Hunter has grown up.
Now imagine the feedback function that would connect his
actions—movements of parts of his body—with the controlled variables for his perceptions of "the car in the proper place on the road, traveling at the legal speed limit.")

Now imagine that Hunter wants to see Sally Ann looking
at him. He believes that if she pays attention to him, she
likes him. What kind of feedback function might allow

Hunter's actions to create the right circumstances in the world for him to see Sally Ann looking at him? Obviously, that function must include Sally Ann. Somehow, Hunter's actions must affect Sally Ann in a way that results in her looking at him. Hunter cannot grab Sally Ann's face and forcefully turn it toward him. If he were to do that, he would treat her like an inanimate object, subject only to the physical laws of lineal cause-and-effect. He would be treating her like a rock that he can pick up and move about as he pleases. If he were to treat Sally Ann that way, it would disturb many of her controlled perceptions, and she would counteract his actions. What is he to do?

All he can do is try to "catch her attention" and hope that she looks his way. In Chapter 2, that is what he does, and that is what she does. Hunter's feedback function runs from his mouth ("Sally Ann, psst! Hi!"), through the air, into Sally Ann's auditory system, and so on, through whatever must happen in her brain for her to decide to look toward Hunter and then to actually look his way. That is a very complex feedback function, with many places where something might happen that would prevent Hunter from seeing the result he wants. His feedback function includes another person, who always acts to control her own perceptions.

Now imagine Mrs. Johnson and her intention to perceive a quiet classroom, which, to her, implies that all of the students are busily studying their assigned lessons. What is the feedback function through which her actions might produce the perceptions she intends? It must run from her actions, through the perceptual processes of each of the students, through the processes by which each of them controls his or her own perceptions, and back out through their actions that affect the environment, which Mrs. Johnson perceives. That is an *extremely* complex feedback function! Imagine all of the places where something might happen, or not happen, so that Mrs. Johnson perceives something other than what she wants!

What can Mrs. Johnson do when she perceives Hunter doing something other than what she wants? Like Hunter with Sally Ann, Mrs. Johnson cannot grab Hunter and force him to do what she wants. That would be treating him like a rock. Instead, she must rely on other means. Like all educators, she undoubtedly learned many techniques to manage, or "control," students' behavior in her classroom. She probably learned that she must teach students to control their actions, by first controlling their actions for them. However, all techniques that are designed to control children's actions assume that they are like inanimate objects, subject to physical laws of lineal cause-and-effect. The techniques include cause-effect practices like delivering reinforcers, levels, and points; creating environments designed to meet students' needs; restructuring students' cognitions; and drugging students whose "brains are defective" and whose "behaviors are out of control." All of those cause-effect techniques are designed around the mistaken idea that children control their own actions, and that, in an emergency, teachers can step in and control their actions for them. But students don't control their actions. Instead, their actions vary any way necessary so that the students can control their own perceptions. If, in her attempts to control students' actions, Mrs. Johnson disturbs too many of the perceptions they control, then they will act to oppose her effects on those perceptions. I am sure that, from time to time, many educators have encountered exactly that outcome, when they applied traditional techniques for "behavior management."

One more point about feedback functions. One person, acting with the best intentions, might intrude into another person's feedback function to help him or her control perceptions, without first being invited to do so. In that case, his actions are likely to disturb her perceptions, and she will then try to counteract his effects. He might, with good intentions, hold a door open for a person who is quadriplegic while she goes through in her motorized wheelchair. However, if she intends to perceive herself as capable of passing through that door unassisted, then his actions will disturb that perception, and she will probably oppose him.

If, uninvited, Mrs. Johnson tries to control Hunter's behavior, then he will probably counteract her. In contrast with those two examples, if the woman who is quadriplegic, or Hunter, requests assistance, then the very same actions by the would-be helper probably will not be perceived as disturbing, and there will be no attempt to counteract them. The difference is between being invited to become part of someone's feedback function and intruding into it uninvited.

A hierarchy of controlled perceptions: "Sally Ann, psst! Hi!" Hunter made those sounds, but what actions produced them? Obviously, Hunter's vocal system moved in just the right ways, with the muscles in his face, throat, and respiratory system relaxing and contracting by just the right amounts, in just the right sequences. It is fortunate that we don't need to think about our actions in that much detail in order to create the perceptions we want. Like Hunter, all we seem to do is think about what we want to hear, and "it just happens." Hunter's utterances began when he wanted Sally Ann to look at him. That was what he wanted to perceive, but instead he perceived her working on her spelling lesson. There was a discrepancy between what he wanted to perceive and what he did perceive. He needed to act, but how? He decided to whisper to her, but he did not perceive himself doing that. (Another discrepancy.) To do so, he needed to perceive his mouth moving a certain way and his breath exhaling in a peculiar sequence, but that was not what he perceived. (Another discrepancy.) To do so, he needed to sense the muscles in his face and respiratory system relaxing and contracting in a particular sequence, but that is not what he perceived. (Another discrepancy.) To do so, he needed to sense increases and decreases in the tensions of individual fibers in his muscles. When that happened, he produced the sounds that he intended to hear.

I just described a hierarchy of perceptions, which is an important feature of PCT. I started at the top, with Hunter's intention to perceive Sally Ann looking at him, and worked my way down to rapid changes in the tensions of muscles in Hunter's respiratory system. When I worked down the hierarchy, I described *how* Hunter eventually produced his actions. A discrepancy (error signal) between intended perceptions and actual perceptions at a higher level became the specification for the intended perception at the next level down in the hierarchy. Finally, at the lowest level, the signals descending from the level above specified the states of muscle fibers that Hunter's nervous system should be sensing, and the states of the muscle fibers changed. Changes in the muscle fibers created his actions. Moving down the perceptual hierarchy explains *how* specific actions occur. In this case, Hunter's specific actions produced the perceptions of his own whisper that he intended to hear.

If we start at the bottom of the hierarchy, with the actions, and work our way up, we see *why* things happen at each level. The muscle tensions occur to produce perceptions of certain forces (specified by error signals from the level above), which occur to produce perceptions of certain movements (specified by error signals from the level above), which occur to produce perceptions of certain sounds (specified by error signals from the level above), which occur to produce perceptions of a specific utterance (specified by error signals from the level above), which occurs (so Hunter hopes!) to produce certain visual perceptions of Sally Ann looking at him. Actually, Ed's description of events in Chapter 2 implies that there is at least one more level above the level where Hunter perceives Sally Ann looking at him. For some reason, Hunter wants to experience affection from Sally Ann, and he believes that when she looks at him, it means she cares about him. Hunter wants to perceive Sally Ann showing affection; to perceive affection, he wants to perceive her looking at him, and so on, back down the hierarchy.

What about Mrs. Johnson's actions? Why did they occur? We heard her say, "Hunter, please stop talking." Again, certain muscle tensions, to produce certain forces, to produce certain movements, to produce certain sounds, to produce a certain utterance ... and then what? Why that *particular* utterance? To produce a perception of Hunter behaving the way Mrs. Johnson thought he should, to perceive a quiet classroom with all students "on task," to perceive herself as a competent and responsible educator. If Mrs. Johnson acts with the intent of controlling Hunter's actions, she sets herself up for him to counteract her, or, as Skinnerian behaviorists would say, to counter-control her.

Hunter whispered to control his perceptions of affection. Mrs. Johnson spoke to control her perceptions of herself as a competent professional person. Do you see why, in PCT, we say that a person's actions, which we perceive from the outside, are not what the person is doing?

Reorganization: Hunter acted to perceive affection from Sally Ann, but his actions also disturbed perceptions controlled by other students and by Mrs. Johnson. Those kinds of actions probably work to control his perceptions in other settings, but in the classroom, they produce unintended consequences for other people and for Hunter. What will happen when Hunter discovers that he can no longer control those perceptions, in that setting, by those kinds of actions? He must find new ways to control his perceptions, or he must select new perceptions to control. In either case, there will be a period during which he senses that some of his important perceptions have gone out of control. Hunter will experience a process that PCT identifies as "reorganization," in which a person tries new ways of controlling, or new perceptions to control, until something works. There is no automatic way to accomplish the end result in a specified time. Often, the selection of new actions, or new perceptions, is random. Sometimes, the person uses a strategy for change that has worked before, or another person might try to guide him through the process. Either way, no one else can make the person suddenly know which new perceptions to control, or how to control them. Sometimes the person reorganizes quickly and easily, but often the process involves a lengthy private struggle.

A student, who for years has successfully used disruption as a way to control the actions of his educators and parents, sometimes struggles for a long time when he encounters adults who use RTP. Adults no longer try to control the student's actions, so he has lost his ability to resist their disturbing attempts at control. When they stop trying to control him, he can no longer control them in return. Techniques that have helped the student control his perceptions of himself as a person no longer work. He experiences large discrepancies between what he wants to perceive and what he does perceive. He might persist in his old ways of acting for quite a while, before he reorganizes.

It is often difficult for an adult to watch a child struggle to learn new perceptions to control, or new ways to control perceptions. Sometimes, with the best of intentions, the adult will "reach into the child's feedback function" and try to help. Frequently, the unintended consequences of those attempts by the adult are resistance and counter-control from the child, and the end of reorganization by the child. The child has discovered that old ways of controlling still work after all, and that there is no further need to reorganize.

Think about Mrs. Johnson. If she is like most educators, when she first declared as an education major, she was taught that she could, and *should*, control students' actions in her classroom. Alternatively, she might have been taught that she, and only she, should create an environment in her classroom that will meet all of the "needs" of all of the students in the room, all at the same time. As a professional person, undoubtedly she was evaluated for her ability to control students' behavior, or to meet their needs. If she is like most teachers, she has experienced the frustration that goes with those impossible assignments. Now we know why those traditional cause-and-effect techniques for discipline do not work: their creators incorrectly assumed that people control their own actions, and that, through clever strategies, one person can come to control another's actions. Now we know that people act to control their own perceptions, not their actions, and that when one person attempts to control another's actions, the controllee will experience disturbance and will counteract it.

Imagine that, after all of her training, and all of her experience using traditional discipline techniques, Mrs. Johnson decides to use RTP. She understands, beyond doubt, that the traditional procedures do not work, but they are all she knows. They are "in her bones." They are the programmatic techniques by which she deals with problems whenever she perceives them. She follows those programs in order to maintain her perceptions of herself as a competent professional person. (In PCT, "programs of action" and "perceptions of the kind of person I am" are at the highest levels in the perceptual hierarchy.) Now Mrs. Johnson hears Ed Ford saying that people do not control their own actions, much less any other person's actions. She learns about a procedure that does not rely on those mistaken notions—one that instead treats students and educators alike as controllers of their own perceptions. She is trying to abandon old (failed) actions that were intended to control her perceptions in the classroom. She is trying to learn new perceptions to control, and new ways to control them.

What is a likely consequence of her endeavor? *Reorganization.* A feeling that "things have gone out of control." (As if they ever were "under control"!) Sometimes, the "loss of control" during reorganization feels so uncomfortable that a person "reverts to the old ways"; but the old ways don't work, so going back to them feels even worse than reorganizing. In that case, the person is likely to press on through the uncertainties of reorganization. Or perhaps the person prefers the familiar discomfort of the failed old ways to the unfamiliar discomfort associated with the (temporary) process of reorganization. In that case, the person might abandon the new ways and return to the comfort of familiar misery.

Putting it all together: How do the ideas in this chapter fit with those in Chapter 2? Hunter wants to perceive Sally Ann as caring for him, but she is studying. He experiences a perceptual discrepancy that drives his actions to change so as to affect Sally Ann, attempting to alter what he sees her doing. The first time he whispers to Sally Ann, she looks at him and smiles, and he believes she cares for him. But Sally Ann intends to perceive herself working on her spelling exercise. She counteracts his disturbance by looking back at the lesson. Hunter whispers again, but this time, unintentionally, his sounds disturb perceptions controlled by Mrs. Johnson and other students. Mrs. Johnson speaks to Hunter in order to counteract the disturbance his actions produced to her perceptions of the state of the classroom, which is part of her perception of herself as a professional person. Hunter stops whispering, and Mrs. Johnson goes back to what she was doing. She assumes that the quiet room signifies that all students are busily at work on their spelling lesson, but Hunter is not. He changes his actions in order to control his perceptions of Sally Ann without disturbing Mrs. Johnson: he writes a note to pass to Sally Ann. I am sure you can imagine several ways to continue the story.

Mrs. Johnson might decide that she is tired of using traditional techniques for controlling students' behavior— techniques that result in students counter-controlling her. She might try to learn RTP, which acknowledges that people control their perceptions, not their actions, and that no person can control the actions of another. If she starts using RTP, Mrs. Johnson is trying to change some aspects of the highest levels in her hierarchy of perceptions. She probably will experience the uncertainties of reorganization. So will any students who learned to counter-control her when she was using traditional kinds of discipline. She and her students will learn new ways to control their perceptions without unnecessarily disturbing others, and new ways to resolve conflicts that unavoidably occur when they disturb one another from time to time. (See chapters 9, 18, and 20.)

Conclusion: In this chapter, I have introduced a few concepts from PCT. I hope that this introduction, along with the ideas in Chapter 2, helps you to appreciate that the theory of behavior behind RTP is different from the theories behind other discipline programs. The traditional theories begin with the assumption that behavior is controlled by forces in the environment or in the brain. In PCT, behavior is identified as the means by which people control their own perceptions of the world. Traditional theories and perceptual control theory differ in many ways, and so do the discipline programs that grow out of them.

It is not easy to learn a new theory, especially when it is as different from traditional theories as is PCT. If you wonder whether you should make the effort to reorganize your thinking around PCT, look at the other chapters in the second part of this book. Examine the descriptions of *results* of RTP as expressed by people who experienced those results. Many of those people are learning PCT. By doing so, they are learning principles that help them to understand whether certain practices are consistent with PCT. They do not need to ask Ed Ford, in every case, whether they are "doing the right thing."

A friendly word of caution: Reorganization around the principles of PCT is not something that most people accomplish in a day or two. Bill Powers, who originated PCT, has been at it since the 1950s. I have been at it since 1973, and Ed Ford since 1982. All of us are trying to undo many years of earlier training, which was grounded in mistaken ideas about lineal cause-and-effect that have been part of Western culture for a few hundred years. We all have a long way to go, but we can already see some of the benefits of making the effort.

PCT References

William T. Powers, *Making Sense of Behavior: The Meaning of Control*, Benchmark Publications, New Canaan, CT, 1998. (A non-technical general introduction.)

W. T. Bourbon, "Perceptual Control Theory," in H. L. Roitblat and J-A. Meyer, eds., *Comparative Approaches to*

Cognitive Science, MIT Press/Bradford Books, Cambridge, MA, 1995. (A semi-technical introduction and survey of PCT research.)

Richard J. Robertson and William T. Powers, eds., *Introduction to Modern Psychology: The Control Theory View*, Benchmark Publications, New Canaan, CT, 1998. (A college-level textbook.)

Hetty van de Rijt and Frans Plooij, *Why They Cry: Understanding Child Development in the First Year*, Thorsons/HarperCollins, London, 1992. (PCT in a new interpretation of infant and child development.)

William T. Powers, *Behavior: The Control of Perception*, Aldine, Chicago, 1973. (The seminal book on PCT; a modern classic.)

William T. Powers, *Living Control Systems*, Benchmark Publications, New Canaan, CT, 1989. (A collection of previously published writings.)

William T. Powers, *Living Control Systems II*, Benchmark Publications, New Canaan, CT, 1992. (A collection of previously unpublished writings.)

Richard S. Marken, *Mind Readings: Experimental Studies of Purpose*, Life Learning Associates, Los Angeles, CA, 1990. (A collection of papers on PCT experimental studies.)

Philip Runkel, *Casting Nets and Testing Specimens: Two Grand Methods of Psychology*, Praeger, New York, 1990. (A modern masterpiece about proper uses, and abuses, of research designs. Identifies the place of PCT in the broad context of behavioral and social research.)

A Personal Afterword

Jake Jacobs is a good friend and a probation officer with the Maricopa County Probation Department, serving the greater Phoenix metropolitan area. Several years ago, he asked me if I would conduct group meetings with adults on probation. Since then, I have conducted meetings both with older mixed groups of men and women and with young men aged 19 through 22 who have been through a 120-day prison boot camp—a shock-treatment experience intended to "knock some sense into them" and to help them develop more disciplined lives, in the hope that they would straighten out their lives while still young.

One evening at a meeting with older men and women, I asked the question, "Do you think people are really responsible for what they do?" The response was unanimous. "Yes, you know when you're doing wrong" and "Absolutely." Acting as devil's advocate, I asked if the community where people grew up, or how their parents treated them, or whether they'd lived where a lot of gangs could influence them would make a difference in terms of responsibility: "Couldn't people from such an environment be excused for what they had done?" One of the longtime offenders, who had been in and out of prison for most of his life, summed up the response of the group: "You know when you're doing wrong, there's something inside of you that tells you it's wrong."

The same reaction came from the young offenders who had been through the boot camp training. They all agreed that each of us is responsible for our actions. "You know it's wrong, but you gotta do what you gotta do," one said.

In conducting student class discussion demonstrations

for school districts throughout the country, I've asked the same question to elementary, middle, and high school children. Recently, I met with a group of eighth grade children at the East Palo Alto Middle School in California. They all agreed that people are responsible for what they do, regardless of who tries to influence them. One young man, Marcus, seemed to sum it up for the group. "Something inside you tells you you're doing wrong."

There seems to be a tendency in schools and elsewhere to blame something outside children for their actions. Courts and juries excuse people who have admitted doing wrongful acts but have claimed no control at the time they committed the crimes. It seems that the very people you would expect to agree with this idea are the ones I have found who, to a person, believe that everyone is responsible for what they do. Even the Judeo-Christian values that permeated our God-centered lives when I was a child seem to remind us of the truth that yes, we are responsible for what we do, regardless of where we came from or what has happened to us. Those in our culture who have turned away from these values have also turned away from the principles which form the foundation of respect for the rights of others.

The respect for laws and rules which allows people to live in harmony with each other finds its basis in the values and beliefs of our ancestors. To quote from the Declaration of Independence: "We hold these truths to be self-evident, that all men are created equal, that they are endowed by their Creator with certain unalienable Rights, that among these are Life, Liberty, and the pursuit of Happiness."

If we don't respect the source of those rights, then we lose what those rights give us—the safety and protection that comes from the assurance that others respect *our* rights. And that's what teaching responsible thinking should do: it should teach children to accept the responsibility for respecting the rights of others. It is only then that we will be able to live in harmony with each other, not only at home and at school, but within the community at large.

Appendix 1
Responsible Thinking Process Card

To receive three copies of the 3" by 5" card reproduced here, send a stamped self-addressed envelope to Ed Ford & Associates, 10209 N. 56th St., Scottsdale, AZ 85253.

RESPONSIBLE THINKING PROCESS

A discipline program that creates mutual respect
by Edward E. Ford - based on perceptual control theory
from his book - **Discipline for Home and School**

For children to succeed they must believe you care about them, that you have confidence in their ability to solve problems, and they must experience mutual respect. The stronger the relationship, the easier it is to resolve differences. If done in a calm, respectful environment, this responsible thinking process can help build that relationship. It also teaches self-discipline through responsible thinking. Ask questions in a calm, respectful, curious voice. Never yell or tell, always ask. Avoid excuses by not asking why.

- **WHAT ARE YOU DOING?**
- **WHAT ARE THE RULES?** or **IS THAT O.K.?**
- **WHAT HAPPENS WHEN YOU BREAK THE RULES?**
- **IS THIS WHAT YOU WANT TO HAPPEN?**
- **WHERE DO YOU WANT TO BE?** or
- **WHAT DO YOU WANT TO DO NOW?**
- **WHAT WILL HAPPEN IF YOU DISRUPT AGAIN?**

WHEN CHILDREN AVOID DEALING WITH YOU

If they avoid answering a question, repeat it. If they persist in not dealing with you, then ask - - -

DO YOU WANT TO WORK AT THIS OR NOT?

If they continue to avoid dealing with you, or, if after settling down, they again begin to disrupt, it means they don't want to follow the rules and have chosen to go to a restricted area. Then you say . . .

I SEE YOU HAVE CHOSEN TO LEAVE.

Once you have said this, never back down. The child must leave at once and go to a restricted area. Once they decide they want to return and obey the rules, they must be taught how to create a detailed plan, and how to use this plan to negotiate with the person in charge of where they were disrupting.

TEACH CHILDREN HOW TO CREATE AN EFFECTIVE PLAN

This process helps them organize their thinking and teaches them how to create successful plans. It builds the self-discipline and self-confidence necessary to successfully resolve future conflicts.

1. Establish a small, single, specific area for improvement.
2. Set a measurable goal to help with feedback.
3. Help them think through then explain a precise, detailed action plan on how they're going to achieve their measurable goal.
4. Create a chart or monitor form as an aid to establishing feedback.
5. Find someone to whom you can report your progress. (continued on back)

These questions may help when creating a plan:

HOW ARE YOU GOING TO DEAL WITH THIS PROBLEM THE NEXT TIME IT HAPPENS?

WHAT WILL HAPPEN IF YOU SUCCEED?

CREATE MUTUAL RESPECT WHILE NEGOTIATING PLANS

The following questions should help you evaluate how well you are teaching this process:

1. Do you always give your child adequate time to discuss her plan?
2. Do you suggest alternatives when the plan is unacceptable?
3. Are you modeling the social skills you expect to see in your child?
4. Does negotiating improve your relationship with your child?
5. Does your child perceive you as wanting him to succeed?
6. When you tell a child anything, who is doing the thinking? When you ask, who is doing the thinking? Are you teaching your child to think?

QUALITY TIME: THE KEY TO A STRONG RELATIONSHIP

LOVE - Willingness to spend quality time every day alone with another no matter how your partner behaves and without trying to control the other person.

CRITERIA FOR QUALITY TIME

1. DO ACTIVITIES THAT PROMOTE AWARENESS OF EACH OTHER AND CREATE PLEASURE THROUGH MUTUAL EFFORT.

such as:	not:
playing games	watching TV
exercising together	going to the movies
working in a business or at home	just being together
doing projects or hobbies	taking a drive
dancing one-on-one	listening to music
taking a walk or a bike ride	watching others

2. DO QUALITY TIME ACTIVITIES ALONE TOGETHER, NOT WITH OTHERS.
3. DO YOUR ACTIVITIES ON A REGULAR BASIS.
   A minimum goal should be at least 30 to 40 minutes per day, five to six days a week. Minimum time with children, 20 minutes per day.

To guarantee a close intimacy, both must be totally committed to spending quality time alone together on a regular basis. To make sure quality time becomes a habit, create a plan. (see other side)

QUALITY TIME ILLUSIONS - Eating together, talking together, and physical intimacy - these activities do not create strong relationships, they can only enhance a committed love that already exists.

Brandt Publishing / Ed Ford & Associates
10209 N. 56th St., Scottsdale, Arizona 85253 Ph. 602-991-4860

Appendix 2
Additional Resources

RTP on the Internet

A responsible thinking process site is maintained on the World Wide Web (`http://www.respthink.com/`). This site includes the latest news on RTP, archived data on the program, and information on how to participate in respthink, the on-going electronic mail discussion group, primarily for educators, that focuses on RTP.

The Control Systems Group

The CSG is a membership organization supporting the understanding of perceptual control systems. Professionals in several disciplines, including biology, psychology, social work, education, engineering, and sociology, are members of the Group. Annual meetings have been held since 1985. For more information, contact CSG, c/o Mary Powers, 73 Ridge Place, CR 510, Durango, CO 81301; phone 303-247-7986.

The CSG site on the World Wide Web can be accessed at `http://www.ed.uiuc.edu/csg/`; this site provides introductory information on perceptual control theory and lists of books and articles about PCT (some available for purchase). The site also provides details on CSGnet, an electronic mail discussion group for individuals who are interested in PCT. CSGnet is a lively forum for sharing ideas, asking questions, and learning about the theory, its implications, and its problems.

Appendix 3
RTP Faculty Initial Assessment Form

RTP FACULTY INITIAL ASSESSMENT FORM

1. Describe your current school discipline program.

_____

_____

2. If you are using a method of discipline in your classroom different from your school program, are you satisfied with your classroom program?   Yes   No Describe your classroom program.

_____

_____

3. Approximately what percentage of your total classroom time do you currently spend with discipline problems or disruptions?

_____

4. Are you held accountable for the behavior of your students when they are in your classroom?   Yes   No

5. Are you held accountable for the number of students you send from your room to the office or elsewhere because of behavior problems?   Yes   No

6. Under your present discipline program, who do you feel is doing most of the work getting your students to control their behavior?   Me   My students

7. What particular skills are your students learning from your present discipline program?

_____

8. Have the number of discipline problems from year to year been decreasing, staying about the same, or increasing?   decreasing   same   increasing

9. Are you satisfied with your current discipline program and the results you are having?   Yes   No

10. Do you currently collect data to support the effectiveness of your program?   Yes   No

11. Please put any additional comments or questions on the other side of this form.

Appendix 4
Letter to Parents Announcing Program

Dear Parents,

Our school has undertaken a new discipline program this year. After reviewing many programs and trying others, we have found the responsible thinking process to be the most effective way for reducing disruption while enhancing the students' ability to resolve problems through the creation of effective plans.

Our Discipline Philosophy

We believe that all students are responsible for their own actions and must be taught to respect the rights of others. Teachers have a right to teach and students have a right to learn in safety. None of the students have a right to disrupt at school, regardless of where they are, especially if they are preventing other students from learning or are threatening the safety and rights of others.

Classroom Rules

No student is allowed to disrupt in class or anywhere else in school, including the school bus. When they do, they are given the choice of remaining where they are and following the rules or going to the responsible thinking classroom (RTC), where they stay until they indicate to the teacher that they are willing to follow the rules. When they do make the choice to leave and go to the RTC because of continued disruptions, they are taught by the RTC teacher how to work out a plan which they will use to negotiate their return with the person who was in charge of wherever they were disrupting. They are only in the RTC for the time they are scheduled with the person in charge of where they were disrupting. Students are permitted to go to all other classes and other areas, such as the cafeteria, recess, and the library, where they are following the rules.

In schools where this program has been successfully adopted, 65% of the students never use the RTC; 25% choose to disrupt only once, and, after making a successful plan for following school rules, never return to the RTC. For the small percentage of students who find difficulty in following rules, we plan to ask their parents to join us here at school so that we may work with them in helping their children to succeed in following school rules.

We have seen this process work in other schools with very positive results. We have found that students develop an increased sense of self-discipline, and, in many cases, their grades improve. This process is based on the book <u>Discipline for Home and School</u> by Edward E. Ford, which grew out of his work in several urban schools in Phoenix, Arizona. We have copies of the book available for you to borrow from our school library, and a video on the program is also available on loan. If you have any questions, please feel free to call us here at school.

Sincerely,